PREACHING BAPTISM

PREACHING BAPTISM

A Practical Guide

JAMES BRADLEY SHUMARD

CHURCH
PUBLISHING
INCORPORATED

Church Publishing
19 East 34th Street
New York, NY 10016
www.churchpublishing.org

Cover design by Joseph Piliero
Cover image by MarioGuti, iStock photo ID: 503169236
Typeset by Nord Compo

Library of Congress Cataloging-in-Publication Data

Names: Shumard, James, author.
Title: Preaching baptism: a practical guide / The Rev. Dr. James Bradley Shumard.
Description: New York, NY: Church Publishing, [2023] | Includes bibliographical references.
Identifiers: LCCN 2023003466 (print) | LCCN 2023003467 (ebook) | ISBN 9781640656369 (paperback) | ISBN 9781640656376 (epub)
Subjects: LCSH: Baptism. | Liturgical preaching.
Classification: LCC BV811.3 .S58 2023 (print) | LCC BV811.3 (ebook) | DDC 234/.161—dc23/eng/20230405
LC record available at https://lccn.loc.gov/2023003466
LC ebook record available at https://lccn.loc.gov/2023003467

Contents

Introduction 1
Why This Book and Why Baptism?

1. Baptism Is a Lifelong Journey 11

2. Baptismal Preaching: Themes from the Catechumenate, Confirmation, and the Reaffirmation of the Baptismal Vows 27

3. Baptismal Vows 33

4. A Quick Guide for Ordinary Sundays with Baptismal Themes as Found in Readings from the Revised Common Lectionary 47

5. Seasonal Preaching and Preaching for Special Occasions 59

6. The Service of Holy Baptism 83

7. Architecture and Accoutrements 121

8. Preaching and Teaching Moments 131

9. The History of Baptism 139

10. Conclusion 161

Appendix A 165
The Question of Open Communion

Appendix B 167
Sample Baptismal Sermons

Bibliography 187

Acknowledgments 195

About the Author 197

This is such an important and timely topic! It's hard to think of a congregation that has not been strengthened by diving into the refreshing waters of baptism. Baptismal values and practices are at the heart both of ministry formation and congregational transformation.

As promised, Shumard focuses on preaching, reviewing the Revised Common Lectionary through the lens of baptism. This valuable resource overflows with opportunities for preaching baptismal themes, yet even more than preaching, the author presents other ways and occasions to highlight baptism. His tone is inviting, enthusiastic, and practically grounded in congregational life.

Baptism, like Eucharist, deeply flows from the generosity of God's love. In my imagination, I hear this author calling out, "Come on in, the water's fine!"

—Fredrica Harris Thompsett,
author of *We Are Theologians* and
Born of Water, Born of Spirit

Introduction

Why This Book and Why Baptism?

Praying shapes believing, which shapes action. Regular weekly worship is the most formative and educational opportunity we have and if we want to communicate something to members of the church it must be done routinely in the primary worship service. Baptisms were normally done in private either in homes or right after the public worship before the 1979 prayer book was used. This meant that the people of God rarely, if ever, saw a baptism or heard the values inherent in the ceremony. The 1979 prayer book rituals and words at a baptism service greatly enhance the theological underpinnings of baptism itself and actively involve the entire congregation in terms of both the Baptismal Covenant and vows, and especially in the resounding "We will!" when asked if congregants will do everything in their power to uphold the newly baptized in their faith.

The purpose of this book is to explore ways to incorporate into the normal Sunday liturgy, through preaching sermons, preaching moments and "preaching actions," the values, signs, symbols, words, and implications of baptism for our life together and in the world—Sunday after Sunday, season after season, year after year—so that these baptismal values *more quickly* become part of how we pray, what we believe and what we do in the world!

We have made great strides toward living into our baptism since the Book of Common Prayer (1979) came into use. Jim Turrell's book *Celebrating the Rites of Initiation*, which addresses performing the ritual in a full and rich manner, Ruth Meyers's *Continuing the Reformation*, and other books that address the history and theology of the rituals and the deeper meanings in the 1979 prayer book lift up the liturgical practices of the service for Holy Baptism. These books encourage us to repeat the themes of baptism through the seasons and feast days and to think and do things large in our ceremonials, using plenty of water and oil and movement. The values of baptism are steadily though ever so slowly seeping into the hearts, souls, and minds of the people in the pews.

There are in the Eucharist and in baptism implications for justice, peace, proclamation, service, formation, and repentance that if truly engaged would send us out to change the world. There is however, a great cognitive, liturgical, and spiritual dissonance between what the Book of Common Prayer and church professionals *say* is important about Eucharist, baptism, and the ministry of the baptized, versus what many people in the pew may think is important.

In an email list for Associated Parishes for Liturgy and Mission, Juan Oliver, the custodian of the Book of Common Prayer, argues that the way we practice in churches today is too "opaque" for most laypeople. He laments over "processions where people don't move; Collects that do not gather . . . a sending that doesn't empower and commission." Oliver wonders that people think the word *symbol* means "not real." However, he also hints at the hope that we can begin to move in the right direction, addressing ways to make our symbols more real to the people, noting that many "can share stories of people who were transformed and brought into the fold by the real thing: bread that was bread, a baptism in enough water to drown in, a Eucharistic full meal, a sending to transform the neighborhood, not a cute thing in sight."[1]

It only makes sense to expand the baptism service if the congregation has embraced these baptismal values, and that will happen if we preach them throughout the year. I wonder though, what would happen if congregations took little steps that turned into bigger steps. As we adjust the liturgies just a bit or combine our services from time to time, then having discussions of baptismal ecclesiology and structure will make more sense. They might even work their way to national church conventions. Imagine what would happen . . .

- *If* advocating baptismal values routinely in the Sunday liturgy became a topic for table talk discussions at clergy conferences, vestry/session/board training conferences, regional or national conventions, or a gathering of seminary deans.
- *If* a seminar on advocating baptismal values routinely in the worship services or enriching the service of baptism itself was offered at

---

1. Juan Oliver, *Advent lections – wreaths*, Associated Parishes Listserv, ap-members@yahoogroups.com, Posted and accessed at 3:16 P.M., December 9, 2009.

seminaries, where seminarians have the time and energy to be creative with preaching and liturgy.

- *If* workshops on enhancing the values of baptism in the liturgy and on baptismal values were offered at continuing education conferences.
- *If* liturgics professors, preaching professors, Christian formation directors, and music directors got in the same room to discuss these ideas.

Our liturgies and our understandings of baptism continue to evolve, and my hope is that the rich symbolism and values that underlie baptism will not simply seep, but fully flow more and more into the hearts and souls, hands and feet, pocketbooks and calendars of the baptized, and influence the continued evolution of our liturgies, our ministries, and our life together as the Body of Christ.

I promise you that if the leaders of worship incorporate some of these ideas into their Sunday liturgies then the people themselves will begin to ask for more! This book is an imaginative and exhaustive resource for those who plan the main worship services and who see baptism as a journey, recognizing that every baptismal service and reference to baptism is "a homily" as much for the adults and children present as it is for those being baptized, in terms of the implications for living out of and into our baptism. I have a plaque on my desk that says these words, popularly attributed to St. Francis: "Preach the Gospel at all times and use words if you have to." We preach the values of baptism in spoken sermons, but also in how we honor baptism with drama and pageantry; where we place the font; how often we splash the people with baptismal waters or recite the vows; and when we take homiletical moments to emphasize a value of baptism.

This book is useful for all mainline denominations seeking to understand and enhance the sacrament of baptism and its implied values, especially since most churches are having fewer and fewer actual baptisms. This book provides historical, liturgical, theological, and practical resources for exploring ways to regularly proclaim, the values, symbols, and actions of baptism.

Holy Baptism and Holy Eucharist are the two primary sacraments of the one holy, catholic—meaning *universal,* not Roman Catholic—and apostolic Church. I hope to, in the words of Fredrica Thompsett, "weave a tapestry of imagination and advice" that supports routinely advocating and promoting the symbols, meanings, values, and implications of baptism and the renewal of baptismal vows.

I will suggest a lot of repetition, for "repeated repetition" is an essential liturgical part of most religious services, whether we are a traditional church or a non-traditional church. We in The Episcopal Church, for example, repeat Holy Communion weekly and repeat the creeds, the Lord's Prayer, and the Confession most every Sunday. We use the same Song of Praise seasonally and the same Eucharistic Prayers over and over again. Regularly repeating the baptismal vows is therefore not out of the realm of liturgical life. Actions speak louder than words, and seasonally asperging (splashing) the people with the waters of baptism while reminding them that they have been sealed by the Holy Spirit in baptism and marked as Christ's own forever has helped my parishioners know that inside themselves.

I would not advise simply reading this from the beginning to the end. There is a whole section in this book on routinely preaching on the values of baptism, but there are also sections, for example, on the history of the theologies and rites of baptism that could be explored.

I have approached this book from the perspective of a priest and rector of a congregation, and I have used as a primary source the service for Holy Baptism (BCP, 299–310) with the Baptismal Covenant and five baptismal vows from the Book of Common Prayer (BCP, 304–305) of The Episcopal Church (TEC). Those from various Christian denominations will most likely be able to identify with most of these rituals and words. The Book of Common Prayer can be found online at the following link: https://www.bcponline.org/.

Many mainline Christian denominations use the *Revised Common Lectionary*, a three-year cycle of readings from Holy Scripture, so I draw upon these readings to discover baptismal preaching theme opportunities. Liturgical seasons and practices are already in place for most mainline denominations and even some of the less liturgical denominations are giving a second look to the value of some liturgical practices, for after all, liturgy—meaning "the work of the people"—is an essential part of Christian education and formation.

This book includes historical, theological, educational, and homiletical (preaching) resources for regularly expounding on baptism and its values and symbols. However, all the preaching on baptism must be supported in actual baptismal services that live up to the preaching with drama, pageantry, and the meanings implicit in the preaching. That is why there is an entire template provided for a "pull out all the stops" baptismal service. Preaching and doing go hand in glove. This book also includes:

- Taking preaching moments in the liturgy and the seasons to talk about baptism.
- Imagining ways to enhance the service of Holy Baptism itself.
- Finding ways and reasons for looking for liturgical moments, places, movements, prayers, and music to preach and teach on baptism

People need to hear sermons on baptism and on its symbols and values more often than during baptisms, because most churches in all mainline denominations are declining in membership and have an older membership, and therefore do not have many infant or adult baptisms. *Additionally, the service for Holy Baptism conveys far more meanings for baptism than can be covered in one sermon on baptism.*

There is in every congregation a significant number of members who have come from other denominations, and they reflect a diversity of theological understandings of baptism (see chapter 9, "The History of Baptism"), which reinforces the need to continuously cover many bases over many Sundays, seasons, and years. This book includes far more suggestions than should be incorporated into any one service. It takes more than talk, teaching, and preaching! It is hoped that this book will become a well of living liturgical water that the ordained minister and the parishioners can tap into under a variety of circumstances.

We preachers, many of whom are also senior pastors of churches and very busy with administration, pastoral care, multiple meetings, and visits, need a resource that provides both impetus and ideas for preaching baptism. Ideally these ideas will lead ministers and the People of God to be more creative themselves. I, for example, have already added suggestions that came from a parishioner, Steve Kurtz (who helped me edit this book), who has been steeped in the baptismal values I have put forth in the liturgy over the last six years. He came up with new ideas that I have incorporated into this book and into my parish life. That is exactly what I hope will happen: that when readers engage with this book, it leads to further engagement with both their congregations and their liturgical leaders.

The impetus for writing this book came out of the experience of church leadership over the last several decades, contrasting their energy advocating for the values and implications of baptism and the Baptismal Covenant and vows at seminars and seminaries, with my experience of people in the pews, who could not name one baptismal vow even immediately after a baptism service. *Unless we repeat over and over again the values and implications of baptism routinely at Sunday services, our people will struggle to incorporate the values of baptism into their day-to-day lives.*

It will take more than what we do in the Sunday liturgy, but if proclaiming by word and deed the values of baptism does not happen in the Sunday liturgy, most parishioners will not soon absorb the values of baptism into their souls. We will need to take many opportunities in and out of worship to preach and teach the underlying values of baptism.

One purpose of this book is to stimulate the imagination of those who preach and plan the primary worship services. It provides useful resources and ideas for routinely and practically preaching the values of baptism. We are all on an ongoing baptismal journey, and baptisms are as much about the whole congregation's lifelong baptismal journey as they are about one who is being baptized. This book provides ideas that will inspire readers to modify or create their own liturgical means to proclaim the values of baptism. *What is included in this book is far more than any one congregation could incorporate at once—but they are all worthy of consideration!*

Weekly liturgical expressions of the values and symbols of baptism are transformative, and what we demonstrate at actual baptisms can be even more powerful. Preaching many sermons on baptism without enhancing the actual service of baptism or the prominence of the font and other pieces of the liturgical furniture, and space and movement, will appear somewhat empty. *Doing one without the other* will not accomplish speeding up the process by which members of the church learn and are formed by baptismal values. The proof is in the pudding, and this has been true in my parish where we have done over forty baptisms in six years in a parish with an average Sunday attendance of just over one hundred.

Congregations that choose to go on this adventure will be able to test the waters, wade in the waters, or jump in the waters. This resource, at its richest, includes some aspect of each of the following:

1. Regularly including the five vows each Sunday, following the Nicene Creed.
2. Congregations viewing a service of Holy Baptism with as much energy and celebration as any other special events in the life of the congregations, such as ordinations.
3. Routinely preaching on baptism.
4. Routinely offering "The Renewal of Baptismal Vows" (BCP, 292–294) and commissioning ministries throughout the year that relate to a particular vow.
5. Making the connection between each vow and a particular liturgical season.
6. Structuring church ministries and ministry reviews around the vows.
7. Congregations viewing formation, education, fellowship, and spirituality in the context of the first two baptismal vows, and with the other three vows relating to how we live in the community and world.
8. Exploring space, time and movement and what it says about the importance of baptism and baptismal values.

There are limitless liturgical ways, in addition to baptism services themselves, that we can help parishioners inwardly digest baptismal imagery, baptismal ecclesiology, baptismal theology, baptismal ethics, and baptismal ministry. We can do this in our liturgies, meetings, preaching, and teaching. We can do it in our structures, our ministries, and in our work and play. We do it "when [we] lie down and when [we] get up" (Deut. 11:19 NIV).

Some suggestions for the liturgy will be simple and non-threatening to laity and clergy in a congregation that wants to dip its toes into the waters of baptismal imagery. For example, a congregation may simply print some information in their bulletin that draws notice to baptismal themes, or they could renew their baptismal vows on the Sundays recommended for baptisms in the BCP. Commissioning various ministries that are congruent with a particular baptismal vow in a particular season should not cause much of a stir.

Other suggestions might require a significant change or even paradigm shift for congregations that want to or have already immersed themselves in the values of baptism. For example, the dean of the cathedral in Phila-delphia, Richard Giles, removed pews and altar rails, moved furniture (this would be anathema to so many in the pews!) and had the entire congrega-tion process at various times from font to pulpit to altar.[2] There are offer-ings here to pique the interest of almost anyone who is in charge of planning worship and ministry and wanting to address the dissonance between what we say and do regarding baptism, in the liturgy, the church, and the world.

This book attempts to integrate liturgy—both words and actions—sermons, church architecture and furniture, church structure and polity, and liturgical seasons, as well as daily life in the home, office, school, and world, all within the context of the symbols and values that underlie bap-tism. It is hoped the more that congregations, dioceses, and national gath-erings begin to think of their life together in the context of an ongoing baptismal journey that what we say and what we do might be more in sync. The theory is that if regional and national church bodies more fully engage these concepts or something similar for a significant amount of time, then mainline Christians will be reminded of their baptism every time they:

- Attend services that mark transitions in life such as ordinations, wed-dings, and funerals.
- Receive their call to baptismal ministry at vestry meetings when deci-sions are measured against the baptismal vows.
- Notice a particular baptismal vow has become a focal point in the liturgy for the new liturgical season or when particular ministries are commissioned that relate to that baptismal vow.
- Participate in a festive baptism with their congregation.
- Are reminded of their own baptism by the certificate hanging in their rooms, by the sacred vessels of water in their homes, and by the cards they receive in the mail celebrating anniversary dates of their baptism.
- Hear sermons preached on baptism throughout each year and every year, from generation to generation.

Maybe then one day when a member of the congregation hears that there is a baptism coming up, they will respond, "A baptism! I think I

---

2. Read any of Richard Giles's books included in the Bibliography.

will invite my friends from work!" and "Baptisms are so beautiful and powerful!"

I can tell you through personal experience as a leader who focuses upon baptism year-round that it has been transformational for my parishes. The people are getting it! This is more baptisms than I had officiated at in the previous twenty years serving as a rector of other churches—large, medium, and small. I find that as I continue to sprinkle the congregation with baptismal water throughout the church year, repeating a short homily, "*Remember* you have been sealed by the Holy Spirit in Baptism and marked as Christ's own forever!" that they are responding in so many ways, whether bowing or repeating the words or asking to be baptized. I recently had a veteran ask to be baptized as soon as possible after he witnessed the baptism of a baby. He struggles with guilt and he understood on a deep level the cleansing act of baptism. People are learning and understanding the baptismal vows as we recite them routinely. Adults and children are asking to be baptized as they experience the drama and pageantry at baptisms and when I am preaching and teaching on baptism. Transformation does take place.

We Episcopalians have made great strides toward living into our baptism since the current prayer book came into use in 1979. The values and symbols of baptism are steadily seeping into the hearts, souls, and minds of the people in the pews, and the purpose of this book is *to accelerate* the rate at which our people absorb the meanings of baptism. This will make a difference in the life of the congregation, and you can trust me! I am a doctor twice over!

The Reverend Dr. "Dr. Give Me the Good News"
James B. Shumard†

Grant, we beseech thee, Almighty God, that the words which we have heard [and read] this Day with our outward ears [and our eyes], may, through thy grace, be so grafted inwardly in our hearts, that they may bring forth in us, the fruit of good living, to the honor and praise of thy name; through Jesus Christ our Lord. Amen. (BCP, 834)

CHAPTER 1

Baptism Is a Lifelong Journey

Grant, Lord God, to all who have been baptized into the death and resurrection of your Son Jesus Christ, that, as we put away the old life of sin, so we may be renewed in the spirit of our minds, and live in righteousness and true holiness; through Jesus Christ our Lord, who lives and reigns with you, in the unity of the Holy Spirit, One God, now and forever!

A Prayer for all Baptized Christians[1]

For baptism, itself is the liturgical and sacramental center out of which we live; it is the watery Spirit-filled womb and tomb to which we are called to return time and time again to find a welcome place in our displaced lives. Indeed, the spiritual journey in Christ is a journey of both place and displacement, a journey of death and resurrection, of birthing pangs and the bringing forth of new life and the paradigm for all this is most certainly baptism.[2]

Maxwell Johnson

Lex Orandi, Lex Credendi, Lex Vivendi

I am not convinced that the deeper meanings and implications of the sacraments of Holy Communion and Baptism have yet seeped into the core of the life and faith of the average baptized churchgoer in such ways as to move us clearly beyond coming to a worship service "for solace only and not for strength; for pardon only, and not for renewal" (excerpt from Eucharistic Prayer C, BCP, 372).

I always expect the first question that a Presbyterian will ask me after attending our services will be, "What do Episcopalians

---

1. *The Book of Common Prayer* (New York: Seabury Press, 1979), 252.
2. Maxwell Johnson, *The Rites of Christian Initiation* (Collegeville, MN: The Liturgical Press), 1999.

believe?" My response is "Come worship with us for thirty years and together we might find out the answer to your question." Traditional Protestants, with a primary focus upon preaching, come from a more doctrinal background, where professing what you believe is crucial to their identity. Anglicans (those denominations such as Episcopalians, who originated in the Church of England) believe that how we pray forms our beliefs, and whatever we pray and do regularly in the Sunday Eucharist shapes our spiritual and credal DNA. Scholars use the Latin terms *lex orandi*—the law of praying—and *lex credendi*—the law of believing—meaning that the way we pray shapes the way we believe. We could add that the baptismal vows can reflect *lex vivendi*—the way we live in the world as a result of praying and believing.[3]

Professor Leonel Mitchell, one of many who helped form the rites of initiation in the Book of Common Prayer, words it this way:

In simple language this means that what we believe is both determined by and expressed in what we say and sing in our worship and the texts of its prayers and hymns are often a truer guide to the actual faith of a Christian community than a study of its theological textbooks. Historically this has been especially true of the Anglican Church.[4]

A 'recent' example of how what we do regularly in the liturgy affects us can be seen in The Episcopal Church's (TEC) decision to adopt the Book of Common Prayer (BCP) for use in 1979. It had baptism and Eucharist at its core. Today, Episcopalians will often say, "I do not feel I have been to church unless I receive Holy Communion!" This is a dramatic change for Episcopalians who grew up under the previous prayer book, when we usually only had Holy Communion once a month. I remember dreading it

---

3. Ruth Meyers, *Baptism, and Ministry, Liturgical Studies One* (New York: The Church Hymnal Corporation, 1994), 12. Quoted in James Bradley Shumard, *A Baptismal Model for Ministry in the Episcopal Church, Connecting Liturgy, Baptism and Ministry Year-Round in Ways which are Congruent with the Book of Common Prayer in Order to Remind the Baptized of Their Baptismal Ministry* (Cambridge: Episcopal Divinity School, 2010), 5.

4. Leonel Mitchell, *Liturgical Change: How Much Do We Need?* (New York: Seabury Press, Inc., 1975), 6.

because the service was longer! We have come a long way in incorporating Holy Communion into our spiritual DNA, yet have a long way to go to understand the value and values of baptism in a similar fashion, especially since there are so few baptisms in the majority of not only Episcopal churches, but in mainline churches.

Catechesis/instruction is still important, and preparation of young people for confirmation used to be one opportunity to learn the implication of baptism, yet many have forgotten what they learned in classes, so they need constant refreshers. I cannot remember anything I learned in confirmation classes other than reciting the Nicene Creed, the Lord's Prayer, and the Ten Commandments. Regardless, with so few young people in churches today those confirmation rites come along rarely. There will be mentioned in this book many opportunities to renew our own Baptismal Covenant other than at confirmation.

Regularly reciting the five baptismal vows each Sunday; routinely replacing the Nicene Creed with The Renewal of Baptismal Vows (BCP, 292–294) in the worship service; greatly enhancing the service of Holy Baptism; routinely blessing the water in the font at the beginning of each liturgical season; and routinely splashing the members with the waters of baptism are straightforward and authentic ways to both "preach" and teach the values of baptism. This is not only congruent with the Book of Common Prayer but it aligns with the direction that scholars of worship have been leading us. The late A. Theodore Eastman, bishop of Maryland, said, "If used properly, taken seriously, and followed to its logical conclusion, then the rite of Baptism *could* revolutionize the liturgical, political, educational and missionary life of the Episcopal Church."[5]

This captures the crux of this book. Baptism would take on more significance for the church and in the day-to-day lives of Christians if people experienced a steady diet of sermons of the many aspects of baptism. Unless our worship services continually inform us in words and actions of what is important in baptism, both theologically and practically, then those of us who teach, write, preach, and lead, will be more challenged to help our people understand the meanings of baptism that underlie what we write and say.

That does not mean that there are no other paths or means to spiritual enlightenment that occur outside the context of the liturgy or the church.

---

5. Meyers, ed., *Baptism and Ministry*, ix.

However, for almost all churches, Sunday worship is the one time, space, and place that all of us hold in common.

I have spent a lot of time *wondering* and *wandering* through the baptismal rites of early churches in many different cities and eras, as well as through contemporary rites of baptism in different places. I have also spent a lot of time wondering and wandering through the theologies of writers through the ages. According to Maxwell Johnson, liturgies and theologies varied from city to city, from culture to culture, and even from church to church, just as they do to this very day.[6] These liturgies flowed out of each church's own traditions, from their relationship with Jesus the Christ, and from their responses to other theologians or strands of Christianity. This, of course, would imply that liturgy has been and always will be dynamic, destined to grow and change through future generations. Understanding this history may help free us to wonder about and explore enhancements to the rites for today as they are lived into by each congregation within the context of their place and time . . . and just as it has always been, every church, every congregation will implement it in their own unique ways.

I have also tried to understand those who put together the 1979 Book of Common Prayer. I have personally spoken with two who were involved in forming the rites of initiation in the current prayer book, the late Leonel Mitchell and the late Marion Hatchett. It is clear they wanted to reconnect Holy Baptism and Holy Eucharist as they saw it connected in the early churches, and wanted to see them as central to our liturgical life together. The fact that Holy Communion has become more important to members of The Episcopal Church since we stopped offering it only sporadically is the inspiration for moving in a similar direction with baptism, both in terms of regular engagement and in prominence.

Those who put the 1979 Book of Common Prayer (BCP) together knew that distributing the Holy Eucharist every Sunday was a key transformational addition to Episcopal worship, not just because they researched church history but because they felt this was a crucial part of our spiritual growth. Christians—and especially denominations that have Holy Communion every Sunday—have absorbed on various levels the comfort and power of Holy Eucharist.

---

6. Johnson, *The Rites*, 41.

The value of baptism as a sacrament and its transformational and moral implications has not fully seeped into the minds of the people in the pews as well as Holy Communion has, and that is probably because baptism is not done very often. Years ago, I heard too many times when it was known that there was an upcoming baptism:

"A baptism?"

"That means the service will be longer than usual."

"I think I will stay home!"

Members of my congregation now say they look forward to baptisms and make no comments about the length of the service. Without constant teaching and preaching on baptism, many of the baptized, in my opinion, do not connect with the deep significance of the symbols and values that underlie baptism nearly as much as they connect with the Eucharist.

Constant repetition and reinforcement of Holy Eucharist, along with the prominence of the altar/table, have been effective formation factors in making the Eucharist central to the formative worship experience of current liturgical churches. Both matter! There are words and phrases from the Eucharist, for example, that are part and parcel of being a participant in the liturgy.

- *Do this in remembrance of me.*
- *Lift up your hearts.*
- *The gifts of God for the People of God.*
- *Christ has died. Christ is risen. Christ will come again.*

It is my hope and prayer that by intentionally incorporating aspects of baptism and the baptismal vows into the regular liturgical life of a congregation, as well as into the very structure of the church organization, that any number of words or phrases from the baptismal rite will also become an integral part of the spiritual fabric of anyone who will be, is, or has been a member of a liturgical tradition for some time. The following are some words and phrases that, not only have I found embedded within my heart and theology but that I hope and pray will be sealed into the lifeblood of Christians:

- *You are sealed by the Holy Spirit in Baptism and marked as Christ's own for ever!* (BCP, 308)

- *There is one body and one Spirit . . . One Lord, one Faith, one Baptism . . . One God and Father of all.* (BCP, 299)
- *We thank you, Father for the water of Baptism. In it we are buried with Christ in his death. By it we share in his resurrection. Through it we are reborn by the Holy Spirit.* (BCP, 306)
- *[We] will with God's help:*
  - *continue in the apostles' teaching and fellowship, in the breaking of the bread, and the prayers;*
  - *persevere in resisting evil, and, whenever [we] fall into sin, repent and return to the Lord;*
  - *proclaim by word and example the Good News of God in Christ;*
  - *seek and serve Christ in all persons, loving [our] neighbor as [ourselves];*
  - *strive for justice and peace among all people, and respect the dignity of every human being.* (BCP, 304–305)

Baptism sometimes appears to be one of those "pro forma" things one does while its multi-layered meanings do not sink in very well. I recently heard a candidate for bishop share that he knew he would not see the parents again after a baptism and that it all felt like a charade. I don't believe that. Baptism is not a charade. It is a lifelong journey.

Baptisms, too often, are not treated with much great expectation, preparation, or pomp and circumstance, even though we are welcoming the newest child of God into the kingdom of God! One day near the end of a weekly staff meeting, I heard a rector (pastor) say, "By the way, we have a baptism this Sunday." A staff person responded, "Oh really? Who is getting baptized?" The rector replied, "The Smith baby." Another staff member then merely said, "Oh, that will be nice."

We often teach and preach by what is not taught and not preached, not said and not done. Indeed, to quote Charlie Winters as he tried to get people to talk to each other in church as they awkwardly learned to exchange the Peace, "We taught people nonverbally that they did not need to talk with one another."[7] We have also taught through absence of intentionality

---

7. Shumard, 47.

and absence of continually splashing our people with the waters of baptism, literally, figuratively, and by proclamation, that baptism is not of ongoing importance. However, those in power in the churches have begun to support reaffirming our vows. Note the fourth point in the *Lima Statement* of the *World Council of Churches, Baptism, Eucharist and Ministry*: "Baptism is unrepeatable, *but should constantly be re-affirmed* [my emphasis] during the baptized Christian's 'continuing struggle' and 'continuing experience of Grace.'"[8]

This is an accurate metaphor reminding us of our need to renew our vows regularly and preach baptism systematically year after year, for we need the seasonal reminder to fulfill our vows at different times in our lives.

What we say and do or *do not say or do not do* before, during, and after a baptism oftentimes does not reflect the awesome realties and implications of the theology, ontology, or ecclesiology of baptism or what those who formed the latest Episcopal prayer book intended. Baptism *can be* a wonderful celebration in the life of the congregation and *can be* a "pull out all the stops" liturgy, for it represents numerous foundational truths, any of which could be the sole topic of a sermon:

- Repentance and renunciation of evil and the washing away of sins
- Salvation and new birth
- Incorporation into the Body of Christ
- Christ's death and resurrection and our death and resurrection
- Reception of the Holy Spirit
- A profession of faith and a commitment to follow Jesus, a call to ministry
- Entry into the communion of saints
- A commitment by the congregation to see that the newly baptized receive all the benefits, rights, and rites befitting an heir to the kingdom!

The good news is that today there is greater attention being given by church professionals to the importance of baptism, the baptismal covenant,

---

8. *Baptism, Eucharist and Ministry*, 25th Anniversary Printing, Faith and Order Paper No. 111 (Geneva: World Council of Churches, 2007), 2–7.

and to the ministry of the baptized. There were a number of resolutions offered at General (National) Convention of The Episcopal Church, for example, that were phrased in the context of the Baptismal Covenant. General (National) Ordination exams questions ask for reflection upon a service for baptism and on the Baptismal Covenant. Those putting together profiles on their churches as they search for new ministers are including references to the Baptismal Covenant.

Fortunately, baptism and Eucharist are a major focus for most mainline denominations and their leadership throughout the church. There are numerous references to the Baptismal Covenant, in church publications, in seminary classes, in parish profiles, and even in national church resolutions. The pope and the archbishop of Canterbury issued a joint statement on October 5, 2016, part of which reads, "Our differences cannot prevent us from recognizing one another as brothers and sisters in Christ by reason of our common baptism."[9]

The ecumenical groups who formed the rites of initiation restored Holy Baptism and Holy Eucharist to their historical place of prominence so that they may once again impact the hearts and minds of the baptized. Authors such as Verna Dozier, Caroline and John Westerhoff, Sheryl Kujawa-Holbrook, Fredrica Thompsett, and others have written with passion about the principles of living into our baptism, baptismal vows, and the ministry of the baptized. Klara Tammany has written with passion on daily ways to living into our baptism, connecting font to hearth.[10] There has also been a substantial increase in the ministry of the baptized and shared ministry as expressed through programs such as "Total Ministry" and "Mutual Ministry."[11]

Baptismal Ministry

Officially, the church defines ministry as actions taken by the baptized, yet many parishioners may still see "ministry" as what the ordained are paid

---

9. *Common Declaration by Pope Francis and Archbishop of Canterbury Justin Welby*, Episcopal News Service: episcopaldigitalnetwork.com, October 5, 2016.

10. Having sacred vessels at home containing blessed water is one of her ideas that is offered elsewhere in this thesis.

11. These models take seriously the ministry of all the baptized and provide ways in which all the people of God share in the ministries of the church. See in the Bibliography the books by Zabriskie and Fenhagen.

to do rather than a ministry to be shared by all the baptized. Many of the assumptions behind what I often say to laity about ministry presumes that they have some understanding of and agreement with the concept of "the priesthood of all believers," when in fact that may often not be the case. We are rarely on the same page when we speak of ministry. We see this lived out dramatically when a congregation is seeking a new rector or pastor. The parishioners often step up to the plate during the interim period and take on ministries, but after the new minister is called, they quickly relinquish them to the ordained minister. It seems that the natural flow is moving the same old way, no matter how much the BCP makes it clear that the ministers are both laity and clergy.[12] I believe that one significant reason for this "dissonance" is that the baptized are not regularly and consistently reminded of the baptismal ministry in the liturgies.

The sacrament of baptism and the symbols and values that underlie it can better become a part of the formation experience of churchgoers if we are able to find appropriate ways to more directly incorporate them into every aspect of our lives together. This can include the actual rite of baptism, the normal Sunday liturgy, the Christian formation programs, the formal structures of the church, the natural transitions of life, major feast days, special liturgies, and rituals in our homes. Protestant Reformed theologian John Vissers offers a vision for the centrality of baptism:

> To be baptized then, is to receive a new existence in Christ, to become a new creation in union with God's crucified Messiah (cf. 2 Cor 5:17); it is to be made in the image for which we were originally created; it is, as the Eastern theologians remind us, to become a person. Baptismal identity creates the basis for Christian worship, discipleship, ethics, spirituality and mission. It embodies our justification, sanctification and vocation. The waters of baptism are the wellspring for a life of faith, hope and love.[13]

This is beautiful and true, yet idealistic, for more than likely many parishioners of any denomination do not fully understand their lives in those terms at any single point in their baptismal spiritual journey. The

---

12. See the catechism in the BCP, 855.

13. Gordon L. Heath and James Dvorak, ed., *Baptism, Historical, Theological and Pastoral Perspectives* (Eugene, OR: Pickwick Publications, 2009), 76–77.

hope is that at different points on the baptismal journey, they will understand much of it.

Some of the baptized have a born-again experience at their baptism or are baptized because of a born-again experience. For some who were baptized as infants, the following might reflect their journey in a more gradual way:

1. An infant is baptized into the church by parents who do not bring the child back until she is of school age.
2. The child attends church until confirmed and, after receiving the car keys, leaves church.
3. The late teen/young twentysomething returns to church Christmas, Easter, and at other visits to parents.
4. The young adult returns to get married and leaves.
5. They return to get their children baptized, each time leaving church for a sojourn in the world.
6. The parents think to themselves when the children get to school age, "Maybe we should return to church and raise our children there."
7. The parents return, bringing their children to church and volunteer in so many areas of ministry that they own the T-shirt, "Been there. Done that!"
8. By the time their youngest has been confirmed, received the car keys, and left church, the parents leave church, having been burned out.
9. The parents, as they grow into their fifties and sixties, begin to think more deeply about their spiritual journey and return to church where they finally remain until they have a great burial service and return to the Lord! Alleluia!

Respecting and anticipating this journey while understanding that living into baptism is a life-long affair may encourage ministers to say, "Yes!" to the "accidental parishioner" who requests that their child be "done." This will mean more baptisms and give the preacher an opportunity to preach on baptism more often, which benefits all who are there. Have we not heard stories of clergy either saying, "No!" to a request for baptism by strangers or long-gone ex-parishioners—who will remain ex-parishioners for the rest of their lives when they get the "No!"—or the minister who forces them into a long set of classes or a catechumenate training program, rather than simply responding, as Philip did to the Ethiopian's request to be baptized, "Yes!"

However, even those who have been baptized or even gone through an intense catechumenate initiation program still may not understand the theologies expressed by theologians or the words said at baptisms. The theological and sacramental depth and meanings underlying baptism as expressed in the service for Holy Baptism in the BCP are too deep and wide to fully permeate any of us in a single service of Holy Baptism or a momentary intense instruction on baptism, but can only grasped by repetition at every stage of our baptismal journeys. For as Catholic priest Bryan Spinks notes,

> Above all, churches are challenged to see the rite of baptism in a wider context of the journey of faith in the community of faith. " . . . In *The Catechism of the Catholic Church*, the section on baptism states that from the time of the apostles, becoming a Christian has been accomplished by a journey and initiation in several stages, and the journey may be covered rapidly or slowly (*Catechism of the Catholic Church*, Liberai Editrice, para. 1229.). The faith required for Baptism is not a perfect or mature faith, but a beginning that is called to develop."[14]

Recognizing that young, previous, or accidental parishioners seeking to get married in the church are actually on that baptismal journey may encourage these minsters to say "Yes!" to their requests as well. God is at work in the lives of all on this spiritual journey, and we had better be ready to respond even as the "accidental and future" parishioners are responding to the nudges of the Holy Spirit in their lives!

More Than Just a Rite

Wherever a parishioner is on their journey, the service for Holy Baptism that they take part in, is about so much more than the rite. Baptism and

---

14. Bryan Spinks, *Reformation and Modern Rituals and Theologies of Baptism, From Luther to Contemporary Practices* (New Haven, CT: Yale University, 2006), 162–163.

the Baptismal Covenant do have transformative power! Too often, many of the liturgical and verbal parts of the baptismal liturgy get lost in the events of the day or overshadowed by some obvious aspects of the ceremony. The preacher is challenged to bring to life *every* aspect of baptism and to help listeners hear, learn, mark, and inwardly digest the appetizers, the main courses, and the desserts.

Preaching on baptism or different theologies of baptism for several Sundays leading up to an actual baptism—especially if baptisms are few and far between—will make the day of the baptism(s) more meaningful and the preacher may not even have to preach on baptism on that Sunday. At my current church, All Saints' Day and Pentecost services with baptisms were as vibrant as our Easter service and attended by 40 percent more people than our normal Sunday attendance. Preaching on the entire baptismal liturgy throughout the year and through the years will aid members to be more fully immersed in the richness, history, and implications of the sacrament of baptism, as well as in the rule of life verbalized in the Baptismal Covenant (BCP, 304–305). All of this may connect baptism to parishioners' personal lives, wherever they are on their baptismal lifelong journey, and help them to hear what the Spirit wants to say to them!

Members learn best what they learn in the liturgy, especially since, on any given Sunday, only a small minority of total adult members attend Sunday school or any educational opportunity. I have not personally met any who have gone through an intense catechumenate—a long training program for adults who want to get baptized. Limiting instruction, catechesis, and preaching to Sunday school or catechumenate classes or actual baptisms could also mean that the newly baptized may be thrown into a congregation that does not fully embrace baptismal values and understandings. This may confuse the newly baptized.

What they have been taught in an intensive baptismal course may happen in baptism, but its implications and meanings will need to be nurtured through proclamation and regular liturgical action in order to sink into their very beings. Paul, for example, was able to make theological references to the images of baptism since the people witnessed baptisms so often. Gerard Kelly, a Roman Catholic theologian, puts it this way: "In other words, baptism frames a whole life, and is not a single moment."[15]

---

15. Heath and Dvorak, 229.

The training, the liturgical event, the preaching, and the Sunday after Sunday references to baptism could be the four-legged bathtub needed to truly get their minds, heart, soul, and body wet.

I have two doctoral theses on baptism, so one might assume that I would call for us to intensify our instruction and preparation for baptism, and yet that is not my recommendation. There have been many books written about the importance of baptism, especially over the last thirty years. The Roman Catholic Church has implemented the RCIA (Rite of Christian Initiation of Adults) classes, and the Episcopal Church is taking the catechumenate far more seriously. John Westerhoff, in his introduction to the Methodist bishop William Willimon's book on baptism, speaks of a long process of formation for those who want to be baptized, including the recommendation that the norm should be that people wait until they are young adults to go through the training and get baptized.[16] This is a great idea, but unfortunately most of those young adults have already left church and do not return for years.

Baptism and its implications are more a curriculum for life and living than a one-time training experience. Yet despite the enthusiasm of scholars, authors, and authorities about the depth of baptismal life, many of our people in the pews still do not appear to "live there." Fortunately, a person on their spiritual pilgrimage may be receptive at any moment. My own story is proof of that.

My Personal Baptismal Journey

Liturgy may make the most important impact on the spiritual lives of parishioners. I say this because I know it to be true in my own life, and I believe that what has been true for me might also be true for so many who either grew up in a liturgical tradition, discovered a liturgical tradition at some other time in their lives, or will be discovering one sooner or later.

I grew up as an Episcopalian and cannot remember missing a single Sunday in church. However, I cannot remember a single sermon nor much of what I learned in Sunday school or confirmation class. It would certainly appear that I got nothing spiritual or religious out of going to church all

---

16. William Willimon, *Remember Who You Are*: *Baptism, a Model for Christian Life* (Nashville: The Upper Room, 1980), 11–13.

those years, for by the time I went to college I considered myself an atheist. I did continue to sporadically attend church, though. However, I eventually had a deeply spiritual experience in my early twenties, whereupon I was surprised to discover stories and "theologies" from scripture and church flooding up from the recesses of my mind. They suddenly made sense to me. Years of hearing them in church must have slipped into my unconscious mind, like a recording played while I slept. I began to experience the joy and peace that passes understanding that I had long heard about in church, and, like the sacrament of baptism, this has been indissoluble since those early days, despite many trials and tribulations.

This is all to say that as I look back at my years of apparently sitting passively through many liturgies, I realize that I was unconsciously or perhaps subconsciously soaking up stories and ways of thinking, praying, and being, which blossomed in my life after this "born again" experience. The constant repetition worked! If the liturgy came alive to me—and this was from the "boring" 1928 prayer book service—how much more will this formation happen if children today grow up in church hearing, seeing, and being regularly splashed with the waters of baptism?

The deeper implications of baptism took on new meanings to me, and what I had learned in the liturgy gave me language to express it. I truly experienced that my old self had died and my new "self" had risen with Christ: I felt "found" and loved by the Creator of the universe. I identified with passing through my own Red Sea of slavery to freedom. The community around me supported me in my faith and set my life on a path to serve God and change the world, exactly how it is spoken of and expected in the baptism liturgy. I would say that the essence of the five baptismal vows was what I thought I had to do in my life, though the new prayer book had not even been written at the time, nor were the five baptismal vows (which are only in the 1979 prayer book) said at my own baptism or confirmation.

This brings me to a very important point. *The Holy Spirit is the One who lives and moves and has its being inside each and every one of us, and within each liturgy, regardless of denomination.* Conversion and transformation happen because of God, not because we tinker with the liturgy. I pray that we and the liturgy simply keep up with the mission of God.

The values of baptism will only take hold and blossom as God makes it so. *Our liturgy is the nurturing soil in which we the people of*

God are planted. The liturgy gives us language and form in which to engage our faith, to grow in faith, to be born into the faith, to be raised in the faith, and then maybe to be born again into the faith. Everything we do in the liturgy is formational, and anything we can do to enhance that experience is a gift to the people of God. This is one reason that ministers would do well to share their personal journeys from the pulpit and invite members of the church to share their own baptismal and liturgical journeys from the pulpit from time to time. Baptism and liturgy are personal.

Therefore, this book is an offering, a gift of thanksgiving for:

- What God has done in my life and in churches
- What God has done in the life of Thomas Cranmer, the author of the first Anglican prayer books
- What God has done in the lives of the twentieth-century "prayer book reformers"
- What God has done and is doing in the lives of today's reformers
- And what God has done and is doing in the lives of the authors who so eloquently share and open up the experience of baptism for the rest of us

My Prayer

My prayer is that together we can unwrap and fully use the gift of baptism that has been handed down to us through the ages and given more immediately to us by those who revised our prayer book. May we further their reformation and adjustments and "perfections;" support the symbols and values and beauty of our historic rites of Holy Baptism and Holy Eucharist; and finally, remember that "There is One Body, one Spirit; There is one hope in God's call to us; One Lord, one Faith, one Baptism; One God and Father of all" (BCP, 299).

Questions for Reflection

1. Does your personal baptismal journey reflect the "in and out of church" journey mentioned above? If not, how does it differ?

2. Is there in your congregation or your experience a "cognitive dissonance" between the importance the prayer book puts on baptism and the importance that you or your congregation put on it? Why do you think that is?

3. How many baptisms does your congregation usually have in a five-year period?

4. Are people around you excited when they hear there will be a baptism? Are *you*?

5. Can you name the five baptismal vows off the top of your head?

CHAPTER 2

Baptismal Preaching: Themes from the Catechumenate, Confirmation, and the Reaffirmation of the Baptismal Vows

I have said earlier that I do not put much emphasis on classes for those to be baptized or confirmed, because I think this kind of catechesis is most effective when brought routinely into the regular Sunday service. The opening line in the catechumenate program in the *Book of Occasional Services* begins: "The systematic instruction and formation of its catechumens is a solemn responsibility of the Christian Community."[1] Seeing baptism as a journey, I would simply substitute "all its members" for "its catechumens." That is why I believe most catechesis needs to take place in the worship service itself.

The sacrament of confirmation is under much scrutiny these days, and I recently heard a bishop say that confirmation is a sacrament looking for a reason to exist. Confirmation is basically a reaffirmation of our baptism and baptismal vows in the presence of a bishop, and I certainly hope bishops who read this book would begin to splash the waters of baptism over the entire congregation at services of confirmation, reminding them of their own baptisms.

I recently was on a pilgrimage to the Holy Land with our bishop and many other pilgrims, where we witnessed baptisms at the river Jordan. The

---

1. *The Book of Occasional Services* (New York: Church Hymnal Corporation), 112–124.

bishop and I were speaking about "believer's baptism," where people who had been baptized as infants wanted to experience being submerged in the waters of baptism. Knowing that "once baptized, always baptized" was the belief of most mainline denominations, we wondered how to instruct persons who wanted this experience.

It became clear that the Renewal of Vows from page 292 in the BCP would be the appropriate "service" for a believer's baptism. What brought this to mind was one powerful image of baptism in the Jordan. We stopped what we were doing to watch a gentleman be baptized. He was quite eager and a bit afraid about the experience and was about to go under by himself, when the minister stopped him and said he must answer some questions first, such as,

"Do you accept Jesus as your Lord and Savior?"

"Do you renounce evil?"

"Do you turn to the Lord?"

Then the minister dunked him three times in the name of the Father, the Son, and the Holy Spirit. We were all moved by this experience.

I can imagine standing in a body of water with someone who wanted to experience a "believer's baptism," going through the "Renewal of Vows," and, as the minster prepares to submerge the already baptized three times, saying what I say every time I splash the congregation during the renewing of our baptismal vows: "Remember (first submersion) you have been sealed by the Holy Spirit in baptism (second submersion) and marked as Christ's own forever!" (third submersion). I in fact did say these words by the Jordan as I splashed our pilgrims with water from the river.

There are unique and self-contained themes for preaching included in the confirmation rites of mainline denominations, when baptized members reaffirm what happened at their baptism and their commitment to a life of ministry. There is an introduction to the service of Holy Baptism in various worship books that offers many potential baptismal themes for sermons, and the following are some suggested preaching themes and/or topics that I have pulled out of those programs. One could preach on any of these themes through the year or several of them throughout a liturgical season such as Lent.

There are also many preaching themes proclaimed in the introductions to baptism in books of worship and, in the following, I have used the ones in the Presbyterian book of worship.[2] The variety of themes is a reminder of how deep and wide the symbolism and reality of baptism is. I find that I need to be reminded of them, and in fact this week I have an adult baptism to oversee, which is a suitable time to review the symbols of baptism before the entire congregation. In this case I will be baptizing a veteran, so I will focus upon the cleansing act of baptism. We want to be aware of each unique context in which a baptism takes place. For example, I would not take this extensive path for an infant baptism. We preachers need to be reminded of each theme, as well, so here are some of those themes:

Baptism is a seal of our incorporation into Jesus Christ, into the Body of Christ. This is the meaning most Christians share, though a few see it as joining their specific local church or their particular denomination. Most mainline denominations see baptism in the broader context of joining the Body of Christ, present, past, and future.

During an actual baptism, some may also experience the communion of saints, that conviction that we are standing in the waters of the Jordan river with John the Baptist and Jesus and all the saints are represented in the waters of baptism.

Through the gift of baptism, we are dead to sin and alive to God in Jesus Christ. Since the fourth and fifth centuries, when Augustine developed the doctrine of original sin, most mainline denominations have accepted this understanding and it was believed that baptism washed away original sin and "got us into heaven." That is why so many nurses, for example, would often do emergency baptisms.

However, this doctrine is routinely questioned, especially by mystics. The issue of original sin was questioned "all over again for the first time" in Matthew Fox's book *Original Blessing*. Having studied the conclusions Augustine came to in dealing with his understanding of Pelagius's writings, Augustine solidified his doctrine of original sin in debating Pelagius, who said we had the capacity to choose good, especially as he observed the corruption of Rome. Augustine believed we could do nothing good without God's help.

---

2. *Book of Common Worship* (Louisville, KY: Westminster John Knox Press, 2018), 403–404.

Sometimes on my sermons on baptism, I will give some lip service to the doctrine of original sin, though there is no Old Testament support for the doctrine of original sin and very little in the New Testament. However, for all practical purposes, we human beings too often act as sinners. When my wife leaves the room and says to me, "Do not eat those fresh baked cookies that you have been smelling all morning," what do you think I will do? The doctrine of original sin and salvation coming through baptism is worth questioning, but let us remember that the criminal on the cross was not baptized, yet in faith he asked Jesus to be remembered in Jesus's kingdom and Jesus said, "Today you will be with me in paradise."

Baptism brings cleansing, pardon, and renewal. Baptism reminds us that God has been offering this cleansing sacrament throughout our relationships with God. Baptism is a cleansing. No matter what sins we have committed or omitted, and no matter what sins we will commit or omit, our sins are removed, and as said in Psalm 103:12 (BCP, 734), "As far as the east is from the west, so far has he removed our sins from us. Isaiah (1:18) also says, "If your sins are like scarlet, will they become like snow?" Psalm 51:8 says, "Purge me from my sin, and I shall be pure; wash me and I shall be clean indeed" (BCP, 656) This is a different cleansing than the concept of cleansing us from original sin.

Just as water washes the exterior body, baptismal waters clean the internal soul. Regardless of our guilt and/or responsibility for the sins, Jesus died and rose from the dead for the sin of the whole world, and this is enacted in the sacrament of baptism itself, where we are reminded that we die to sin and rise with Christ in the waters of baptism.

The Holy Spirit is given in baptism. Paul recognized that the reception of the Holy Spirit was part and parcel of baptism. That is why we offer the laying on of hands, and why I remind the people so often that we have been sealed by the Holy Spirit in baptism. It is the Holy Spirit that empowers us to keep the Covenant. We are anointed with the Holy Spirit and infused with God's power to love and forgive, both ourselves and others.

Baptism is a sign of God's covenant with us and our covenant with God. God has been reaching out to us in a covenantal relationship since the beginning. We signify that covenant and the New Covenant in baptism and Eucharist.

The waters of baptism are linked to the waters of creation, the flood, and the Exodus. The images from Genesis and Exodus have been incorporated into the sacrament of baptism from the beginning. God's spirit hovered over the waters in Creation, delivered Israel from slavery to freedom through the waters of the Red Sea, and delivered Noah and his family through the waters of the great flood.

Baptism also represents God's call to justice and righteousness, rolling down like a mighty stream. This is a reference to Amos's call to the people of God to care for the widow, the helpless, the powerless, the aliens among us. Our modern-day prophet, Rev. Dr. Martin Luther King Jr., refers to Amos in his famous "I have a dream" speech, which reflects the dreams contained in baptism and the dreams contained within Jesus's preaching the kingdom of God. This reminds us that we are being baptized and cleansed for service to God and one another.

Baptism enacts and seals what the word proclaims: God's redeeming grace offered to all people. Baptism reflects that God is doing the work of baptism. We baptize babies not knowing how they will turn out, for good or for bad, but still recognizing and giving them to God's unfailing grace for all time.

Baptism is at once God's gift of Grace, God's means of Grace, and God's call to respond to that grace. It is all about God and our response to God's gifts and calls. Baptism is more about what God does in baptism than what we do or what the church does. God forgives. God sends the Holy Spirit. God cleanses us. God empowers us. God calls us and sends us forth.

When we are baptized, we are made one with Christ, with one another, and with the Church in every time and every place. Nothing can separate us for the love of God in Christ Jesus. Baptism reminds all of us who have been baptized of that reality.

Through baptism, Jesus Christ calls us to repentance, faithfulness, and discipleship. Repentance is a key word Peter uses for his first sermon, where three thousand people were baptized. We will ask every candidate for baptism if they, with God's help, will renounce the evil ways of the world. These themes cover most of the aspects of baptism that Christians have shared, to one degree and another, though not all of them at the same time.

Questions for Reflection

1. How would you address someone coming to you who has already been baptized, but asking for the experience of a believer's baptism?
2. What are your thoughts on the rite of confirmation?

CHAPTER 3

Baptismal Vows

A Blueprint for Living Out the Values of Baptism

The baptismal vows, which conclude the Baptismal Covenant[1] in the Episcopal prayer book, may be summed up in Jesus's commandment, "Love God and love one another as I have loved you." Jesus laid down his life for us in love and we are called to do the same. Baptism reminds us of what God has done for us in Christ, and our baptismal vows are part of our response to God's Grace in Christ. The baptismal vows reflect, as my friend Steve Kurtz says, "a blueprint for a way of life for Christians." They are a way of life, *lex vivendi,* a model for ministry and discipleship that includes the way of the cross and the way of the Spirit. The five vows provide a path for how we want to behave as a response to what we say we believe. Here are some ways to do that.

Incorporate the Five Vows Immediately after the Nicene or Apostles' Creed

The starting point for suggestions and the simplest way to incorporate the five vows into the normal Sunday worship is to add them immediately after the Nicene Creed. The vows represent what we promise to do as a result of what we believe. Implementing this practice would go a long way toward fulfilling the purpose of this book.

Many liturgical traditions recite either the Nicene or Apostles' Creed almost every single Sunday, as well as the Confession and Lord's Prayer, among other repetitive pieces of the liturgy. Repeating ourselves appears to be an essential part of the liturgical tradition, so repeating the five vows immediately after reciting the creeds should fit in with our tradition.

---

1. The entire Baptismal Covenant can be found in appendix B.

The suggestion here is that the leader include a transitional invitation to the people to recite their vows, like at a wedding. Actually reciting the vows will better serve people remembering them than simply responding with, "We will, with God's help," as we do during the service for Holy Baptism. I do this every time we recite the vows, and it works. Here is a template for instituting this practice.

The People: [Nicene or Apostles' Creed]

Leader: Now that we have professed our faith with our lips,
let us profess what we will do with our lives:
Please repeat after me:
We will with God's help, continue in the apostles' teaching and fellowship, the breaking of the bread and the prayers.
We will with God's help, persevere in resisting evil and whenever we fall into sin, repent and return to the Lord.
We will with God's help, proclaim by word and example the Good News of God in Christ.
We will with God's help, seek and serve Christ in all persons, loving our neighbors as ourselves.
We will with God's help, strive for justice and peace among all people, and respect the dignity of every human being!

Leader: May God give us the desire, the will and ability to fulfill these vows.

Unpacking and Preaching the Vows

We should do a bit of reflection on the vows before we go any further in suggestions for renewing them in the liturgy. Each vow can reflect a season and specific ministries in the church.

Participation: The First Vow

Will you continue in the apostles' teaching and fellowship, in the breaking of the bread, and the prayers?

The first vow, which is almost a direct quote from the Acts of the Apostles, describes why and how the first Christians gathered; it comes to us as a package, so leaving part or parts of the package out can decrease the effectiveness of the whole. Most churches do well with prayer and the breaking of the bread (worshipping together), and statistics show that those who gather for fellowship, whether in small groups or at a thirty-minute coffee hour, fare better. Annual reports indicate that many church members fall short in showing up for worship. Even fewer show up for Sunday school or coffee hour. I believe that takes away from some of the intensity and power of worship. Regular attendance, fellowship, and education are all part of this vow, and we must work harder to fulfill it.

Our understanding of the "fellowship" and "education" part of the first baptismal vow is quite weak. Having coffee with friends for five minutes after the service and listening to the reading of scriptures in church are not what Luke meant in Acts 2, when he wrote of continuing in the "apostles' teaching and fellowship."

Remembering that liturgy is the "work of the people," can we not work just a bit harder for just a few more minutes? In my congregation we provide for blessing of birthdays, anniversaries, and other special moments with humor and spiritual depth. People are invited from time to time to share from the lectern, offering any spiritual insights they may have. This is a way to share our lives a bit more and learn something in the process. We bold special or more important parts of the readings so that the congregation can read along, and I give brief context and explanation before or even during some readings. Parishioners tell me they pay more attention when I do this, and it becomes part of my teaching moments.

When is the liturgy—the work of the people—over? We clergy are still working very hard during coffee hour. "Oh, Father Jim, you must meet this new young couple immediately!" We clergy make our rounds and the adrenaline is still running through our veins until we finally lock the last door and drive home in exhaustion. Maybe it is time that *all* the baptized left church a bit more exhausted from their efforts. Maybe it is time we became a bit more intentional about fellowship and education and what it means. After all, even for some of us extroverts, it is so easy to gravitate to the people we know rather than getting to know strangers. We should focus on creating an atmosphere of fellowship before, during, and after the worship service.

Introducing fellowship at structured times makes it easier for clergy and parishioners to leave their comfort zones. A non-threatening time to consider introducing new fellowship opportunities would be whenever a congregation chooses to reaffirm their baptismal vows. On those Sundays, the procession out could move all the way to the parish hall, where some intentional community building program structure was in place.

I recommend asking a parish leader to count people off in groups of five or more around one table to discuss a question related to the baptismal vow theme of the day. This gets people speaking with one another and speaking about baptism. Newcomers who began attending since the last "fellowship day" could also be introduced to the small group at this time. If conversation is slow to start, various "community building" exercises could be done in order to help people find commonalities among themselves. Some educational material could be presented and then discussed.

It is difficult for many of us to walk up to someone we do not know—or worse yet, have known by face for years but not yet learned their name—and begin a conversation. The important part of this is that all of it would be intentionally connected to the first baptismal vow. The bottom line is that Sunday worship with some education and fellowship within the worship service itself can add both to the spiritual depth and interrelational depth of the worship experience.

The beginning of the season after Pentecost (Ordinary Time) would be a good time to preach on liturgy, stewardship, fellowship, education, or the many ministries of the congregation.

Repentance and Forgiveness: The Second Vow

Will you persevere in resisting evil, and whenever you fall into sin, repent and return to the Lord?

Confessing sins and repenting of them is part and parcel of the preaching of John the Baptist, Jesus, Peter, and Paul. Lent is an obvious season to focus upon this vow and preaching on the confession would be appropriate. Speaking of the temptation to participate in evil, whether it be listening to racially insensitive jokes, liking critical comments on social media, or giving in to hatred and judgment, could be part of this theme. Using new confessions that address specific issues of the day and hit close to home can bring the confession to life. If, for example, there has been recent conflict in the church, then a specific reference to that conflict could be included in the general confession or prayers of the people, with silence to let the people sit with whatever feelings they might have. Follow this with a robust teaching on the forgiveness of God just before absolution is pronounced. Confessions around our consumerism, our isolation, our abuse of creation, could be added. A confession that includes a call to action might be effective.

Lent would be an appropriate season to preach on a rule of life that will help all persevere in resisting evil. Historically the season of Lent has been more focused upon individuals, but this season could also be a time to examine the church community and explore any reconciliation that needs to take place or to face temptations—toward complacency, liturgical snobbery, or our inability to live the vows as a church. This could "relieve" rectors of teaching an inquirers' class, and the entire congregation could benefit from refresher courses from time to time.

Lent is still a season when many churchgoers do go the extra mile to learn a bit more about their faith and to practice it in a bit more disciplined manner. A preacher could divide up the three temptations Jesus faced— power, magic, and immediate satisfaction, or as so many say, "giving them a fish instead of teaching them to fish." Congregants can be encouraged to consider: Where are we working for our spiritual food? Where are we working to serve the needy? Where are we working to proclaim resurrection and new life to others?

Proclamation: The Third Vow

Will you proclaim by word and example the Good News of God in Christ?

Proclaiming by deed through outreach, and being a good person, appears to be the way many Christians choose to proclaim the gospel. Yet for some, it is a challenge to share their personal faith with others. I hear members say it is a private matter, or that they are afraid of being judged as a fundamentalist. Focusing on the third baptismal vow would be a good time to help our people learn how to share their faith stories about God and Jesus and the Holy Spirit in appropriate ways. Inviting parishioners to share their faith stories from the pulpit is one way to do this.

A preacher could share stories of how to proclaim the Good News for members of the denomination, including their own efforts—or their own failures—to do so. Celebrating church outreach while adding some words of life would be another example of proclaiming by both word and deed. Offering to pray for someone, rather than simply saying, "I will be thinking of you," is another example. Encouraging parishioners on a routine basis to do both may open some doors in their lives to attempt it.

Easter season is a time for reflecting on and focusing upon ways to verbalize the faith within ourselves and to others. Presiding Bishop Michael Curry[2] invited Episcopalians to learn to do this as a way of becoming a missional church. He is quite aware that Episcopalians and many Christians are shy about proclaiming their faith out loud and he is trying to help parishioners become comfortable verbalizing our faith stories to ourselves and others.

Service: The Fourth Vow

Will you seek and serve Christ in all persons, loving your neighbor as yourself?

Serving others is something most Christians can identify with and attempt to do. Feeding the poor, clothing the naked, and sheltering the homeless are part of this, and sharing examples of how members of the parish are doing this will reinforce keeping this vow. Understanding that each human being is created in the image of God might be a way for us to learn to respect the voices that differ from ours, and may even irritate us. We are all walking sacraments of God's grace, so we should try to see one another in that light.

Epiphany could be a season to focus upon the fourth vow, seeking and serving Christ outside the church and possibly in the digital universe, providing "stars" for seekers. It is a time to provide signs and wonders that the world can see so it might be drawn to Jesus. Our faith is our greatest gift to be offered to the spiritually homeless and thirsty. Christopher Duraisingh

---

2. Curry was elected presiding bishop in 2015.

suggests seeing the font as the exit of the church rather than the entrance, believing that the church should be seen primarily as an armory for training for mission.[3]

Social Justice: The Fifth Vow

Will you strive for justice and peace among all people, and respect the dignity of every human being?

I have observed that many suburban churches have a difficult time, as institutions, striving for justice and peace, and we need to find ways to keep this vow as a congregation and as individuals in this politically divisive culture. How can a congregation find a social justice cause that can unite them?[4] How can a congregation intentionally encourage its membership to individually become advocates, while not only respecting the dignity of human beings outside the church, but respecting the dignity of every member's opinion in the church?

Advent and Christmas, when we hear the prophets call for justice in the kingdom of God, may be a season to focus on justice. Maybe individuals can share what they are doing for justice and peace, or the leaders could provide a time to incorporate a special confession that addresses social justice issues, such as can be found in the Great Litany (BCP, 148) or the Litany of Penitence from the Ash Wednesday service (BCP, 267).

Taking the Vows as a Whole

Considered individually or together, when all five vows are connected to the normal Sunday liturgy they can become a part of our Christian identity and even energize our secular life. They should serve as a focus for a season, and be proclaimed in a variety of ways, including in the Prayers of the People, the Eucharistic Prayer, and the lifting up of specific ministries that relate to that vow.

---

3. As quoted in Shumard, *Baptismal Model for Ministry*, 49.

4. Our parish has been able to agree on ways to help the working poor as one way Republicans and Democrats can come together to help those who are fishing but catching little. Our "Change the World ... One Diaper at a Time" program is about giving a month's supply of diapers to the working poor, which helps hard workers, children, and parents without enabling anyone. This program evolved out of the question "What social justice issue can we unite around?"

Baptismal vows can be incorporated into the promises church boards and regional authorities use as they recruit persons for ministry and evaluate ministries in the congregation, including mutual ministry review, and should factor into the way national church bodies measure the success of resolutions, as well as their impact on congregations and the world. A mutual ministry review of and by the leadership then becomes a way to evaluate both the budget and the life of the congregation based upon how well they are fulfilling those promises, rather than evaluating the performance of the clergy and/or vestry/board. The board will then begin asking questions such as: "How well are we doing as a congregation (as a board, as individuals) in striving for peace and social justice; in seeking and serving Christ in all people; in repenting of evil and returning to the Lord; of proclaiming by word and deed the Good News of God in Christ; and of showing up at church and Sunday school and learning to know and love one another?"

The same can be done for state or regional ministries. The sixty-seventh General Convention of the Episcopal Church, which met in 1984, passed a resolution calling upon dioceses to use the baptismal promises to spearhead evaluation of parishes and missions.[5] Locally, church boards can use the baptismal vows to guide their ministries and encourage parishioners to apply the vows when considering how to structure and evaluate their personal politics and relationships, and their commitments of time, talent, and treasure in the church and in the world.

Imagine a congregation that can see each of their ministries in light of one of the five baptismal vows. Committees might be renamed to reflect each vow: "Formation Ministries," "Spirituality Ministries," "Proclamation Ministries," "Service Ministries," and "Peace and Justice Ministries." What if state or regional governing bodies promoted a baptismal ecclesiology to congregations? What if vestries/boards/sessions were led by consultants to have discussions about the implications of moving toward a baptismal ecclesiology and ministry? Picture state or regional bodies structuring their own commissions and ministries around these same values.

---

5. Donald Chapman, "The Eight Faces of Baptism" (doctor of ministry thesis, Divinity School of Vanderbilt University and the School of Theology of the University of the South, 1984), 14.

Renewal of Baptismal Vows

Renewing baptismal vows can take place outside the context of the formal liturgy, such as at stewardship banquets and the opening meetings of various ministries, committees, vestry retreats or when new vestries first meet. The more often we connect what happens in the liturgy to what happens in the ministries of the parish and world, the better.

Using a version of the Renewal of Baptismal Vows rite (BCP, 292)[6] is at the heart of a baptismal model for ministry. The BCP recommends four Sundays for baptisms in addition to visits from the bishop. Whenever there are no actual baptisms scheduled, the congregations could replace the Nicene Creed with the Renewal of Baptismal Vows. This is suggested in the "additional directions" on page 312 of the BCP. Replacing the Nicene Creed with the renewal of vows for an entire season such as Lent or Easter would work well. In his book *Planning the Church Year*, Leonel Mitchell suggests that the preacher may want to give some introductory words right after the sermon.

The Renewal of Baptismal Vows incorporates the renunciation of evil and renewing a commitment to Jesus Christ, in addition to all that is included in the Baptismal Covenant on pages 304–305. William Palmer Ladd suggested years ago that every "first Sunday" be a rededication day to ministry of all kinds and renewing of our baptismal vows on the first Sunday of each new liturgical season could be done in that spirit.[7]

For those congregations that do not want to radically immerse themselves in renewing baptismal vows, there are other opportunities to return to it, such as the feast day of the congregation or the annual meeting. Renewing baptismal vows at the opening of state, regional, and national conventions would set an appropriate tone for them and provide an

---

6. There is often some confusion with the words "renew" and "reaffirm." The "Renewal of Baptismal Vows" is part of the Easter Vigil service on pages 292–294. It includes in addition to the vows, a question of renunciation of evil, and renewing a commitment to Jesus Christ. The reaffirming of baptismal vows is on pages 303 and 419, and is for those people who were previously baptized but may have stopped attending church for quite a while and now have returned. Finally there is the bidding by the celebrant at the bottom of page 303, which invites all the baptized (the entire congregation) to join with those seeking baptism, confirmation, reception, and reaffirmation of baptismal vows, and "renew our own baptismal covenant." The baptismal covenant is then recited by all.

7. Christopher Irvine, ed., *They Shaped Our Worship* (London: Society for Promoting Christian Knowledge, 1998), 60.

example and support for congregations doing the same. Eventually this may become second nature for all ministries.

Renewal of Baptismal Vows as a United Congregation

Baptism represents our unity in Christ: one faith, one church, one baptism. For churches that typically hold two or more services, offering only one service (if there is space available) whenever there is a baptism or on the Sundays designated for baptisms or the renewal of vows in congregations is an effective way to provide an outward and visible symbol of the values of baptism.[8] Regional and national leaders could intentionally encourage this practice. Bishops often include in their customary the expectation that there will be only one service, space being available, at the visitation, and why.

Of course, the suggestion of having a single united service on a Sunday can stir up some of the strongest objections within some congregations, though many congregations already merge services during the summer. Not only will you hear that the members from the early service may not attend, but people will ask, "What will we do with the children for such a service?"

Would it not be a teaching moment for children and adults to wake up and say, "Why are we going to church at a different time on this day?" Having the service at nine o'clock in the morning would be quite biblical.[9] Combining the services also makes the nave fuller, more festive, and more exciting. Just as many remember Christmas midnight services with a special sense of holiness and mystery, perhaps children will remember baptisms with a special sense of holiness, mystery, and celebration.

The following are suggestions of appropriate times to have one service and/or to routinely renew baptismal vows:

The Entire Easter Season

This of all seasons would be a great unifier. Attendance is traditionally low during this time so everyone could probably fit in the sanctuary. I

---

8. Advance notices of time change should be accounted for in the public as well as within the congregation.

9. The story in Acts 2 has the crowds asking, "Are these people drunk?" Peter responded that they were not, for it was only nine in the morning. After hearing Peter preach, over three thousand were baptized. Now that is a teaching moment!

recommend renewing the baptismal vows in place of the creed every Sunday during Easter season. Consider unpacking Paul's understanding of dying and rising with Christ in baptism, being buried in the waters of baptism, and rising to a new resurrected life. This is especially a time to reflect upon Jesus's resurrection and Great Commission.

The BCP recommends five Sundays to have baptisms—the Baptism of Our Lord (the Sunday after January 6), Easter, Pentecost, All Saints' Day (November 1), and the bishop's visit. These days would be obvious choices for preaching on baptism and renewing the baptismal vows, even if there is no baptism as the BCP recommends on page 312, but there are many more opportunities to be found! The following are suggestions of appropriate times to have one service and/or to routinely renew baptismal vows:

"Fall Kick-Off Sunday"

Typically when Christian education programs begin would be a time to focus on the apostles' teaching and commission all those who minister in Christian formation. (Why, for instance, if Sunday school is open to all, do so many congregations usually commission the teachers only at the later services?)

Annual Congregational Meeting

This is the meeting where business is conducted, the budget is reviewed, vestry members are elected, and the rector/pastor gives the annual report. The rector/pastor may want to report on how well the congregation has lived the baptismal vows. What better time to renew baptismal vows and to review the year in light of having kept those vows? I give my state of the parish as the sermon on that day and always incorporate baptismal values in it.

The First Sunday of Each Liturgical Season

Members will get to at least recognize each other if a vows renewal is performed this often. Each of these Sundays could be a time to focus upon one of the baptismal promises that fits the season, and the ministries related to them would be commissioned at the services. What a teaching moment it could be when the children ask, "Why is this Sunday so different?" and the parent answers, "Don't you remember? We always do this the first Sunday of a new liturgical season." Liturgy is the ultimate Christian formation experience.

Pentecost Sunday

The birthday of the church would *definitely* be a Sunday for the entire congregation to renew their baptismal covenant. It is a time to focus upon being filled with the Holy Spirit, being empowered by the Holy Spirit, being born again, and being anointed into the royal priesthood of all the baptized.

The Feast of the Baptism of Our Lord

The Second Sunday of Epiphany was an appropriate paradigm for baptism in the early church and forms a background for our contemporary baptismal celebration. This could be a time to focus upon being commissioned for ministry at our own baptism, a calling toward the world, and a time to deal with temptation. Clergy and parishioners should ask, "How then shall we serve the Lord?"

People could be reminded that they too have been anointed with the Holy Spirit at baptism for ministry. We were not baptized into the church to remain in the church. We were baptized for ministry beyond our doors. We were baptized, not just for the repentance of sins, but so that we would turn around and follow Jesus, preaching the repentance of sins. We were not sprinkled or immersed with a little bit of water so we would only have a little bit of Jesus in our life, but were sprinkled with the blood of the lamb and made pure as the driven snow so we might be driven by the Holy Spirit into the world, rejoicing in the power of the Spirit.

All Summer, from Pentecost through Kick-Off Sunday

Many congregations already have just one service then, especially since attendance is down. This is also the beginning of Ordinary Time and might be a good season to dress casually. This time, the kids will ask, "Why are we all dressing so casually today?" Children could put an extra dollar in the offering plate since they were dressing casual, much like many schools do on Fridays.

All Saints' Day

Well, that says it all doesn't it? This is a time to focus upon being incorporated into the local body, reminding all of the indissolubility of baptism and that nothing can separate us or our loved ones from the love of God.

Feast Day of the Parish

Preaching on all the vows on the feast day of the parish would be a way to look at the past year together. This is a time to point out how and where the congregation as a whole has been living out of those vows. It may also be a time to challenge the congregation to further live into the vows.

Questions for Reflection

1. Have you ever thought of doing a preaching series on baptism? What topics would you cover?
2. Would it be a struggle to combine services for baptisms? How might you overcome these struggles?

CHAPTER 4

A Quick Guide for Ordinary Sundays with Baptismal Themes as Found in Readings from the Revised Common Lectionary

Preaching Baptism Year-Round, Generation after Generation

Thomas Long quotes Augustine, saying that "The purpose of a sermon is to teach, to delight and to persuade."[1] People's hearts and minds are open while engaging a sermon, and that is significantly different from listening to instruction. It will take *preaching, teaching, and performance* to move congregations toward the deeper meanings of baptism. The best diet for inwardly digesting baptism and its meanings is in regularly tasting from all three of these "food groups," beginning with sermons on Ordinary Sundays.

I have looked through the lectionary readings for all three years and identified readings that relate to the topic of baptism. There are a number of Sundays throughout the three-year cycle that directly refer to baptism. Certain scriptures repeat themselves through the lectionary, and there will be duplicate commentary and duplicate highlighted scriptures. This is done rather than referring the reader to another section, for preachers are very busy and want the information at their fingertips without having to scroll down to other years. The duplication will be noted so the preacher can consider whether repeating this

---

1. Thomas Long, *Preaching from Memory to Hope* (Louisville, KY: Westminster John Knox Press, 2009), 5.

theme the next year. Scriptural quotes are taken from *The New Oxford Annotated Bible* or from *The Revised Common Lectionary, Episcopal Edition*.[2]

The following are suggested Sundays to consider preaching on some aspect of baptism, with relevant scriptural selections from the Episcopal RCL.

Year A

First Sunday after Epiphany, the Baptism of Our Lord

Matthew 3:13–17: "This is my son, the Beloved, with whom I am well pleased." *The Collect*: "Grant that all who are baptized into his Name may keep the covenant they have made, and boldly confess him as Lord and Savior."

God is well pleased with Jesus before he even begins his ministry. Likewise God is well pleased with us before we begin our ministry.

Second Sunday in Lent

John 3:1–17: "Very truly, I tell you, no one can enter the kingdom of God without being born of water and Spirit."

This passage from John is rich in baptismal images, including baptism in water and in the Holy Spirit. This would be a time to preach about the charismatic experience of being baptized in the Holy Spirit, and a time to preach on the understanding that we receive the Holy Spirit in water baptism.

Easter Vigil

Romans 6:3–11: "Do you not know that all of us who have been baptized into Christ Jesus were baptized into his death?"

The Vigil, in light of Good Friday and the Crucifixion, is a perfect time to preach on the experience of our old selves dying with Christ and our new selves rising with Christ.

---

2. *The New Oxford Annotated Bible with Apocrypha, Revised Standard Version* (New York: Oxford University Press), 1977 and *The Revised Common Lectionary, Episcopal Edition, New Revised Standard, 3 Year Cycle*, (Wichita, KS: St. Mark's Press, 1992).

There are so many opportunities to delve into themes and theologies of baptism in the Easter Vigil, for it is the highpoint of the baptismal experience and formation. Whether the preacher preaches homiletic moments after each reading during the Vigil or chooses one or two theological themes for the major sermon, there is plenty to work with in terms of baptism.

Sixth Sunday of Easter

1 Peter 3:13–27: "And baptism, which this prefigured now saves you—not as removal of dirt from the body, but as an appeal to God for good consciences, through the resurrection of Jesus Christ."

Most will probably preach on Paul's address in the Areopagus, but occasionally the preacher may want to preach on First Peter. Note its reference to Noah and the flood, and the righteous dying for the unrighteous.

Pentecost

1 Corinthians 12:3b–13: "For in the one Spirit we were all baptized into one body—Jews or Greeks, slaves or free—and we were all made to drink of one Spirit."

Use the opening acclamation at a baptism service: "There is one faith . . . ." Preach on how baptism unites us despite our division . . . one body, many parts. We are united by the work of Christ in baptism and united in supporting the persons being baptized. This is another reason to have only one service on the day of a baptism.

Trinity Sunday

Matthew 28:16–20: "Go therefore and make disciples of all nations, baptizing them in the name of the Father, and of the Son, and of the Holy Spirit."

Preaching the great commission is a new way to avoid preaching on the Trinity, and an opportunity to focus upon proclaiming and baptizing! An even more important line to have the congregation repeat and memorize is: "And remember I am with you always, to the end of the age." Being baptized and marked as Christ's own forever reminds us that Jesus is with us always.

Proper 7, June 19–June 25

Romans 6:1b–11: "Do you not know that all of us who have been baptized into Christ Jesus were baptized into his death?"

Preach the themes of being united with Christ in his death and united to him in his resurrection, and reasons to behave as the redeemed. The ethics of the baptismal vows could be preached, or dying and rising with Christ, which is Paul's deep understanding of the experience of baptism. Our old self has been crucified with him so that the body of sin may be destroyed. "So you also must consider yourself dead to sin and alive to God in Christ."

Proper 12, Year A, RCL

Romans 8:12–25: "For I am sure that neither death, nor life, nor angels, nor principalities, nor things present, for things to come, nor powers, nor height, nor depth, nor anything else in all creation will be able to separate us from the love of God in Christ Jesus our Lord!"

This reading from Paul is the crescendo in the theological symphony of Paul's Letter to the Romans. His words, "Nothing can separate us from the love of God in Christ Jesus," are an echo of what I say in the baptismal service: "You are sealed by the Holy Spirit in baptism and marked as Christ's own forever, and nothing you or I do can change that—and don't you forget it!"

Neither death nor life nor principalities nor powers, nor faith nor lack of faith, nor belief nor lack of belief, nor morality nor immorality, nor praising God nor cursing God can separate us from the love of God! So many people still believe that their behavior, their faith or lack of faith, negates the results of the work of Christ on the cross; negates the work of Christ being born of a woman, and living, teaching and preaching among us; the work of Christ in rising from the dead and ascending to the Father. Let's get this one straight, people! Nothing can separate you from the love of God, and you are marked as Christ's own forever!

Proper 27, November 6–November 12

Amos 5:18–24 (alternative reading): "I hate, I despise your festivals, and I take no delight in your solemn assemblies. . . . Take away from me the noise of your songs; I will not listen to the melody of your harps. But let justice roll down like waters, and righteousness like an everflowing stream."

As mentioned earlier, this last line is part of Martin Luther King Jr.'s "I have a dream" speech, and it calls us to ask how we are advocating for justice in our culture. This line would be an appropriate refrain to read in the Prayers of the People or in the midst of the reading of Amos.

The fifth baptismal vow speaks of the active verb "striving." The fifth vow calls us out of our silence as a congregation and as individuals to actively seek justice where we see injustice. Sometimes we remain blind to injustice locally and globally. Jesus sends us out to be innocent as doves and wise as serpents. Where are we exercising these spiritual muscles?

These verses from Amos may especially speak to churches who highly value their tradition and liturgy. Many of us are proud of our beautiful worship services, so the graphic nature of the words of Amos can draw us up short. Do we argue more—do we expend more time, energy, and money on our liturgies than we do in time and arguments about how we shall serve the poor? Amos implies that our liturgies can only be pleasing to God if we are serving the poor. Our liturgies will have more intensity and meaning when our ministries have more intensity and meaning.

Year B

First Sunday after Christmas (Years A, B, C)

Galatians 3:23–25, 4:4–7: "... but when the fullness of time had come, God sent his Son, born of a woman, born under the law, in order to redeem those who were under the law, so that we might receive adoption as children."

This is an opportunity to refer to our adoption as children of God through the life, death, and resurrection of Jesus Christ. We speak of being made heirs, calling God "Abba" through the waters of baptism.

First Sunday after Epiphany, the Baptism of Our Lord

Mark 1:4–11: "And just as he was coming up out of the water, he saw... the Spirit descending like a dove upon him. And a voice came from heaven, 'You are my Son, the Beloved; with you I am well pleased.'"

Jesus is water baptized and Spirit baptized, exactly what we say happens in our baptism. We are anointed by the Holy Spirit so we have power to live out of our baptism. Jesus hears the voice calling him Son, and we are made heirs to the kingdom through baptism.

This Sunday is about the Holy Spirit, and we continue that theme in the story from Acts 19:1–7: "When Paul laid his hands upon them, the Holy Spirit came upon them, and they spoke in tongues and prophesied—altogether there were about twelve of them." Paul noticed that something was missing: the Holy Spirit.

This is the time to preach on the anointing of the Holy Spirit and the laying on of hands in baptism. References to Ananias laying hands on Paul to receive healing and the Holy Spirit, would be appropriate as well (Acts 9:17): "He laid his hands on Saul and said, 'Brother Saul, the Lord Jesus, who appeared to you on your way here, has sent me so that you may regain your sight and be filled with the Holy Spirit.'"

Not only does Paul receive his sight, but through the Holy Spirit he receives insight into Christ. A preacher may want to address the concept of being baptized in the Holy Spirit and what that might mean for ministry.

First Sunday in Lent

1 Peter 3:18–22 and *Mark 1:9–15:* "... when God waited patiently in the days of Noah, during the building of the ark, in which a few, that is eight persons, were saved through water. And baptism, which this prefigured, now saves you—not as removal of dirt from the body, but as an appeal to God for a good conscience, through the resurrection of Jesus Christ, who has gone into heaven and is at the right hand of God, with angels, authorities and powers made subject to him."

Wow! A preacher could have a heyday with this in terms of baptism: the flood, the creed (seated at the right hand of the father), and dying and rising with Christ. A reference to Noah is made here and was once part of the imagery of baptism in previous liturgies for baptism. The preacher may speak of salvation in water, the new covenant, deliverance through the waters of the Red Sea, the flood, and baptism. The First Sunday in Lent is always a good time to preach about the temptation not to live out the baptismal covenant, or the implications of being a child of God.

Fifth Sunday of Easter

Acts 8:26–40: "As they were going along the road, they came to some water, and the eunuch said, 'Look here is water! What is to prevent me from being baptized?'"

This is the story of Philip and the Ethiopian, when Philip proclaims the gospel to the unnamed Ethiopian who responds to proclamation with this wonderful, highlighted line of faith. This echoes the criminal on the cross, asking Jesus to remember him when he comes into his kingdom. Once again, along with Peter's question at Cornelius's house, the question of preventing baptism comes up with the author's obvious slant toward not allowing anything or anyone to prevent us baptizing anyone at any time! This is another reason for senior ministers to be willing to baptize on request, regardless of membership or amount of catechesis, keeping in mind the life-long baptismal journey. Preaching on inclusiveness is an obvious choice.

Sixth Sunday of Easter

Acts 10:44–48: "Then Peter said, 'Can anyone withhold the water for baptizing these people who have received the Holy Spirit just as we have?'" No!

Preach about all people being of one Body and one Blood in the waters of baptism, and on being inclusive, for we know that Peter knew in his very question that some would want to give good reason to withhold the water for baptism. I have heard of priests who refuse baptism because applicants are not members, or for other reasons. I baptize on request!

Trinity Sunday

John 3:1–17: "Very truly, I tell you, no one can enter the kingdom of God without being born of water and the Spirit."

The senior minister/pastor/rector who does not have an assistant or guest preacher to help them avoid preaching on the Trinity can still avoid explaining the Trinity by preaching on baptism. The Trinity will be presented and/or experienced rather than explained, for, after all, the doctrine of the Trinity evolved out of the experience of the Trinity. This passage from John is rich in baptismal images, including baptism in water and in the Holy Spirit. The preacher can even recall Jesus's baptism, where the Trinity of the Father, the Son, and the Holy Spirit is overtly presented.

Proper 10, July 10-July 16

Ephesians 1:3–14: "In him you also, when you had heard the word of truth, the gospel of your salvation, and had believed in him, were marked with the seal of the promised Holy Spirit; this is the pledge of our inheritance toward redemption as God's own people, to the praise of his glory."

This passage speaks to so much of what happens in baptism without mentioning the word itself. It includes incorporation into the body, being made an heir, receiving the Holy Spirit, adoption as his children, redemption through the blood, forgiveness of our sins, eschatology, and salvation. The preacher can go anywhere from here!

Proper 13, July 31–August 6

Ephesians 4:1–16: "There is one body, and one Spirit, . . . one Lord, one faith, one baptism, one God and Father of all."

This is the famous scripture that our opening to all baptisms echoes, and it would be an appropriate Sunday to open with the baptismal acclamation: "There is one Body." Consider using this line as a congregational refrain during this reading, and all the other readings from Paul in which he speaks of the many different gifts for ministry and/or of the divisions within the Body.

Year C

First Sunday after Epiphany, the Baptism of Our Lord

Luke 3:.15–17, 21–22: "He will baptize you with the Holy Spirit and fire," or *Acts 8:14–17*: "Then Peter and John laid their hands on them, and they received the Holy Spirit."

The preacher could speak of baptism in the Holy Spirit and fire including Pentecost. The preacher could contrast Jesus's own baptism with baptism in the name of the Father, and of the Son and Holy Spirit, contrasting the judgmental nature of John's baptism and preaching with the transformative nature of our baptism. One difference to note in Luke: where it is said that after Jesus was baptized and while he was praying, the Spirit fell and the voice was heard. Jesus is always praying in Luke.

The quote from Acts offers an opportunity to teach and preach on the laying on of hands to receive the Holy Spirit, which is a crucial part of baptism.

Third Sunday after Epiphany

1 Corinthians 12:12–31a: "For in the one Spirit we are all baptized into one body—Jews or Greeks, slaves or free—and we were all made to drink one Spirit."

Paul is speaking about ecclesiology, the workings and ministries of the church, reminding all that we find our humility and our exaltation in the waters of baptism and the work of Jesus Christ. Preachers will probably want to preach on the many parts of the Body of Christ and could include that we become one body in baptism and that "water is thicker than blood," when it comes to ethnic, social, racial, economic and political parts of the Body.

Fifth Sunday of Easter

Acts 11:1–18: In these verses, Peter is defending his actions in baptizing Cornelius, a gentile, and in fact his whole household. Some see the fact that Peter baptized the entire household as support for infant baptism. I consider the true theme to be inclusiveness in the midst of a strong mind-set of exclusivity and the rigorous ritual demands of the community. This scripture could be preached around social justice, respecting the dignity of every human being, why we perform infant baptisms, or how the gospel kept spreading throughout the known world.

The preacher would do well to remind listeners of the implications of this experience, which is so great that it had to be retold a couple of times in scripture. Not only was Peter worried about having witnesses, but the writer of the gospel wanted to make clear this was the work of God and not Peter. Once again baptism is intimately connected with the coming of the Spirit. The Spirit works as it pleases and is not confined to institutional sacraments.

Seventh Sunday of Easter

Acts 16:16–34: "Sirs, what must I do to be saved? They answered, 'Believe on the Lord Jesus, and you will be saved!'"

This is the story of Paul and Silas being set free in prison through an earthquake, and their proclaiming the gospel to the guard who, along with his entire household, is baptized. The jailer and his whole family are baptized, leading scholars to refer to this story when referencing the baptizing of children. Therefore, it may be an appropriate time to speak about infant baptism.

Infant baptism reminds us that baptism is about the work of God, not about our work. Baptism is about God's having chosen us, not our choosing God. Baptizing infants reminds us that we have no idea how good or bad this baby will grow up to be. It reminds us we are saved by grace and not by works or by faith. Parishioners can be encouraged to ask themselves, "Are we living in such a way that people ask us the secret to living?"

Vigil of Pentecost

Gospel of John: 7:37–39a: "Out of the believer's heart shall flow rivers of living water."

Pentecost is about insight, power, proclamation, conversion, and baptism. Both Acts and the gospel address the coming of the Holy Spirit, and how the Holy Spirit is so intimately connected to giving the apostles something to preach about and empowering them to do so. Preaching on the role of the Holy Spirit in our lives would be appropriate. The falling of the Holy Spirit on the people is intimately connected to our rite of baptism in that we are expected to receive the Holy Spirit in baptism.

In addition, Romans 8:14–17, 22–27, which is read at the Vigil of Pentecost, is a classic Pauline connection to creation; being made children of God, heirs of God, and all about the Holy Spirit.

Proper 7, June 19–June 25

Galatians 3:23–29: "Therefore the law was our disciplinarian until Christ came, so that we might be justified by faith. But now that faith has come, we are no longer subject to a disciplinarian, for in Christ Jesus you are all children of God through faith. As many of you were baptized in Christ have clothed yourselves with Christ. There is no longer Jew or Greek, there is no longer slave or free, there is no longer male or female; for all of you are one in Christ Jesus."

This reading is long, but includes Luther's focal point of being saved by faith, so highlighting that particular line would be an opportunity to preach on how faith impacts our life in Christ. Being clothed in Christ is another theme to develop, and a preacher might speak to the history of having the white robe put on after each baptism. Since the parishioners will have seen this happen many times the image would be clear.

Proper 11, July 17–July 23

Amos 8:1–12: "Hear this, you who trample on the needy, and bring to ruin the poor of the land, saying, 'When will the new moon be over so that we may sell grain; and the sabbath, so that we may offer wheat for sale? We will make the ephah small and the shekel great, and practice deceit with false balances, buying the poor for silver and the needy for a pair of sandals, and selling the sweepings of the wheat.'"

This is one of the more memorable passages from Amos, which presents a good time to address an accusation often leveled at today's Christians: that they behave one way on Sunday and a different way Monday through Friday. Chances are there are few if any in the congregation who are blatantly cheating the poor, but there is no doubt that in our society, the poor pay higher interest rates, and that medical care and taxes take a higher percentage of their spending money than the spending money of the wealthy. This is a time to focus upon the fifth baptismal vow regarding striving for justice and peace. Where are Christians advocating for the poor, not just in sitting on charitable boards, but in advocating with politicians for the poor? Will we with all our influence only use that influence for our own good?

Proper 12, July 24–July 30

Colossians 2:6–15 (16–19): "See to it that no one takes you captive through philosophy and empty deceit, according to human tradition, according to the elemental spirits of the universe and not according to Christ . . . when you were buried with him in baptism, you were also raised with him through faith in the power of God, who raised him from the dead."

Paul is warning his listeners, many of whom were Gentiles, not be deceived by false teaching and useless ceremonies such as circumcision. This may be a time to preach on the Apostles' Creed and the Nicene Creed, however the preacher engages them, for it is held up as the standard from which all other beliefs can be weighed. The preacher can explore the variety of ways that each belief has been interpreted. It is the belief of this author that this orthodox creed needs to be honored and weighed in contrast to the other beliefs that have been being expressed for two thousand years. What are called heresies tend to be truths taken too far at the exclusion of other truths, and many classic heresies are still believed by people in the pew. The church throughout history has tried to suppress these heresies through debate and executions, but they keep popping back up and will continue to do so. We need to honor those and chew on them even as we listen to, meditate upon, and inwardly digest the Nicene and Apostles' Creeds.

Proper 13, July 31–August 6

Colossians 3:1–3: "If you have been raised with Christ, seek the things that are above . . . for you have died, and your life is hidden with Christ in God."

This reading reinforces the themes of dying and rising with Christ, clothing ourselves with a new self, and reinforcing Paul's understanding that there is neither Greek or Jew, circumcised or uncircumcised, barbarian, Scythian, free or slave, but Christ is all in all.

Many listeners may not have had or understood the experience of letting the old self die, so the preacher may want to share their own experience or explicate Paul's experience. If possible, provide examples of ways in which to focus upon the eternal treasures, the things that are above. Preachers who have never had a personal experience with letting an old self die may want to share what that it is like for them to read this passage, as many listeners may be in the same boat.

Questions for Reflection

1. What is your favorite baptismal imagery to preach on?
2. What new themes could you consider for further Sundays?

CHAPTER 5

Seasonal Preaching and Preaching for Special Occasions

As we look at the lectionary, we should also consider the liturgical seasons, which present unique opportunities to share the baptismal gifts with your congregation. Preaching on baptism every Sunday of a liturgical season every couple of cycles emphasizes the importance of baptism, while giving the preacher time to cover the varied aspects of the rite. There are numerous actions and rituals that speak so deeply of baptismal values. The following are just some of them. As you begin to view the lectionary through the lens of baptism, you may begin to identify more on your own.

Preaching Consecutive Sundays During a Season

Every Sunday in Lent

Pastor and seminary professor Melinda Quivik recommends preaching on the implications of baptism throughout Lent,[1] which is considered by some to be a traditional time to prepare for baptism, particularly during the Easter Vigil or Easter service. Taking a long view, a baptismal preaching series could be undertaken every third year or so in the life of a parish. This would serve as a refresher course on baptism for the whole congregation.

---

1. See Melinda Quivik, *Preaching Baptism through Lent*, workingpreacher.org, February 6, 2012.

Every Sunday in Easter Season

It may be that in the routine life of a parish that an occasional entire Easter season could be a time to unpack the implications of baptism in our lives. There is historical precedent for this practice, Quivik notes: "From documents such as Cyril's sermons [of Jerusalem ca. 350–387], liturgical historians suggest that in the early church, the baptismal rite preceded explanation about it."[2] Marion Hatchett, one of the key liturgists involved in the formation of the 1979 Book of Common Prayer, also suggests this, commenting that "Because of the *disciplina arcani,* the discipline of secrecy, the initiates did not learn the meaning of these [baptismal] rites until after their participation."[3] By speaking regularly on baptism throughout the Easter season, preachers can begin to uncover these secrets with their congregations.

Every Sunday in Advent Season

John the Baptist preaches fairness and simplicity, whereas Jesus preaches radical generosity and sacrifice. John tells us to share from surplus and Jesus tells us to give away essentials. This season of shopping and giving, this season of token gifts to the poor, can help contrast John and Jesus. Advent is about "Your Kingdom come on earth as in heaven," yet this is a challenging season for Christians to find ways to strive for justice in church and society. Advent reflects the prophets of the Old Testament in the Magnificat (the Song of Mary, Luke 1:46–55) and the life and words of John the Baptist.

Preachers are warned to stay away from politics and money in the pulpit, yet, like money, Jesus often addresses politics directly. So much in the Gospels shout politics to Jesus's listeners, the first readers of the Gospels and to those of the early church. Calling Jesus "Lord" was an act of treason to Caesar. This is a season of advocacy for the poor and getting right with God ethically and mystically. Advent may be a time to ask the people who or what, on a day-to-day basis, is lord of their life.

---

2. Ibid.
3. Marion J. Hatchett, *Commentary on the American Prayer Book* (San Francisco: Harper Collins, 1980), 254.

Preaching the Baptismal Vows Across the Seasons

Congregations that are familiar with baptismal vows should consider commissioning ministries in the liturgy at different times of the year. This regularly reinforces the values of baptism in the liturgy while publicly encouraging and promoting these ministries in ways that may help call forth new ministries. Congregations may, for example, begin to structure their ministry fairs into five sections based upon the baptismal vows, so visually the parishioners would "see" these vows lived out among themselves. They could host several different ministry fairs each year with the "ministries of the seasonal vow" being the focus.

Below is an example of one possible format for vows that fit the seasons, along with ways to emphasize ministry in connection with both. Some aspect of the baptismal vow that fits the season should be lifted up liturgically, whether through the music, the Eucharistic Prayer, opening words and actions in the liturgy, the Prayers of the People, added collects or prayers, commissioning of ministries that relate to the occasion, or simply through moments of instruction. The first Sunday of each liturgical season should accomplish that. Hanging up banners reflecting the baptismal vows during a particular season might serve as helpful reinforcement.

The Book of Common Prayer encourages creativity and additions by the clergy and people. For example, it allows people to write their own version of the "Prayers of the People," noting "Adaptations or insertions suitable to the occasion may be made," and "The Celebrant may introduce the Prayers with a sentence of invitation related to the occasion, or the season, or the Proper of the Day" (see the rubric on page 383 of the BCP). The celebrant is also allowed to add a concluding collect at the end of the six forms of Prayers of the People offered on pages 383–393 of the BCP.

Additionally, congregations are permitted to model the format of the confession contained in the Ash Wednesday liturgy (The Litany of Penitence on pages 267–269 in the BCP) so that it specifically relates to the baptismal vow of the season. The dismissal could also reflect these vows.

The following are further suggestions for creatively embracing baptismal vows with your congregation throughout the seasons:

Advent and Christmas: The Coming Kingdom of God

Vow *Will you strive for justice and peace among all people, and respect the dignity of every human being?*

Ministries Peace and justice ministries could be commissioned, prayed for, and invited by the congregation to gather around the altar at the Great Thanksgiving. Proclaiming these values in congregations that do not typically advocate for justice might inspire them to do so.

Themes The readings address the coming of the Day of the Lord, the coming of the kingdom of God, etc. They include John's call for ethical living and the Magnificat's warning to the rich. Mary and Joseph struggle with the political power of Rome and Herod.

Classes and Programs Formation could focus upon the words of the Old Testament prophets who advocated for social justice with the people of Israel.

Congregation Vestries could examine how well the congregation and individuals are striving for justice and trying to establish the peaceable kingdom. If there is conflict in the parish, this would be the time to address it before Christmas. The baptized could be led through exercises that examine their daily lives at home, office, and school in the context of justice, fair trade, HIV/AIDS, gender roles and prejudice, carbon footprints, and attitudes toward minorities and other groups that may be ostracized by society.

Epiphany: Reaching beyond the Stars and Doors

Vow *Will you seek and serve Christ in all persons, loving your neighbor as yourself?*

Ministries Evangelism/proclamation and/or service and ecumenical ministries could be a focus. Soup kitchens, mentoring, providing night shelters, serving on non-profit boards, etc., could be commissioned, prayed for, highlighted in the bulletin, and/or they could gather around the altar for the Great Thanksgiving.

Themes Epiphany is a season of seeking and finding. The magi came from afar. Jesus calls his disciples to become fishers of people. The Beatitudes are read, addressing all sorts and conditions of people. We are to be the light of the world, the entire world, not just for our selective community.

Liturgy The Prayers of the People could include prayers to inspire the congregation to seek and serve all people, spelling it out a bit more clearly. Prayers for those who minister and for those who are ministered to could be offered. The dismissal could reflect these concerns and those who are directly involved in these ministries would be invited to bring oblations and gather at the altar, etc. Ministers from other religions could be asked to preach during the liturgy.[4] Ecumenical efforts and celebrations could be a focal point, including praying for denominations that we are in communion with as well as praying for the people of other religions.

Classes and Programs Classes might focus upon learning about other religions, focusing on stories of the great saints from the church and famous figures from other religions.

Congregation The baptized could be given take-home materials to teach them about other religions and other denominations, as well as the history of discrimination against those of other religions in our country and throughout time. This is a good time to talk about community service.

Lent: A Time of Self-examination by Both Individuals and Congregations

Vow *Will you persevere in resisting evil, and, whenever you fall into sin, repent and return to the Lord?*

Ministries Ministries that connect directly to our spirituality could be the focus, such as the Daughters of the King, prayer guilds, Education for Ministry (EfM) classes, and others.

---

4. I, for example, have invited a rabbi to preach on Old Testament stories.

Themes The season of Lent is traditionally a time of personal preparation and a time when people prepare for baptism. It is a season for examining evil both personally and institutionally.

Liturgy More contemplative services and silence in the liturgy would be appropriate. Those responsible for prayer ministries could be prayed for and invited to gather around the altar. Corporate prayers of repentance could be written. A congregation could experiment with prayer stations during the liturgy.

Classes and Programs Formation could focus upon the psalms, for they depict some of our deepest personal emotions as they relate to our spirituality.

Congregations Spiritual training could be offered, including the various historical Christian disciplines. The parish could offer silent retreats, meditation books, renewal speakers, etc. Baptized persons could explore exercises simplifying their lives, their homes, and their expenses.

Easter: Proclamation and Invitation

Vow *Will you proclaim by word and example the Good News of God in Christ?*

Ministries Proclamation ministries, those responsible for evangelism, newcomers, ushering, greeting, communicating, could be commissioned.

Themes This is the season for understanding our faith and the gospel.

Liturgy Preachers might simply add a prayer to the liturgy, "Lord help us learn to share our faith." A congregation might want to reaffirm the Baptismal Covenant in place of the Nicene Creed each Sunday in the Easter season.

Classes and Programs Christian formation (education) could focus on learning the basics of the faith and how each of us incorporates those beliefs into our own faith.

Congregation Members should be prepared to explore their own faith by considering how they might respond to questions posed by the community, such as "When were you saved?" or "What do you think of the theory of 'intelligent design'?" or "Will you pray for me?" This is the season to help the baptized understand their faith enough to verbalize it, at least to themselves if not to others.

Season after Pentecost (Formally Ordinary Time): Daily Life in Christ

Vow *Will you continue in the apostles' teaching and fellowship, in the breaking of the bread, and in the prayers?*

Ministries Formation ministries that are connected directly with worship could be highlighted, as would Christian education, fellowship groups, and many of the other internal groups of the congregation.[5]

Themes This long ordinary season would be time to focus upon the disciplines of church attendance, Christian formation/Christian education, stewardship, the environment, and the liturgy.

Liturgy All the various inward focused ministries, such as worship, altar guild, and fellowship groups could be commissioned on various Sundays, accompanied by the renewal of the baptismal covenant.

Classes and Programs Formation could include a ministry fair that focuses on the internal ministries of the congregations.

Congregation The baptized could be given information that helps them understand the basics of the faith so they can explore how they do or do not currently incorporate it in their lives. Stewardship would certainly be an appropriate focus in the fall.

---

5. I continue to use the word "congregation" rather than "parish," for in certain dioceses, using the word "parish" excludes other congregations that are labeled as "missions."

The Easter Vigil Service

Those who put the BCP together physically placed the Easter Vigil service both at the end of the special liturgies and immediately before the service of Holy Baptism. Many churches do not celebrate the Easter Vigil the night before or the morning of Easter itself, yet this service is rich in tradition and meaning for baptism. There are many ways throughout the year that aspects of the Easter Vigil service can be embraced.

For example, congregations might use the first part of the Vigil for processions in with the Paschal candle, or consider singing all or part of the Exsultet (BCP, 286) at the beginning of services of baptism or services that will include the Renewal of Baptismal Vows within the Easter Vigil service (BCP, 292). Part or all of the Exsultet could be said or chanted as well, after changing a few words regarding night and morning. Certainly, the first part of it (BCP, 286) could easily be adapted for any or all of the services during the Easter season, along with the Renewal of Baptismal Vows. This could add to the drama and pageantry during the season of Easter, which typically can be considered anticlimactic compared with the power and pageantry of Easter morning.

The Liturgy of the Word from the first part of the Easter Vigil (BCP, 288–292) incudes our entire salvation history in scripture. Surely churches would benefit from regularly engaging these readings. In my church we accomplish that during the season of Lent, which is traditionally a preparation time for the Vigil, Easter morning, and for baptisms. We read one of these readings each week during our Lenten mid-week services and reflect upon them. What better way to prepare for Easter!

Other Seasonal Flourishes

The Structure of the Liturgy

One of the beauties of liturgical traditions is that between the intentions of prayer books, missals (Roman Catholic order of worship), and worship guides, and the intentions of those who plan liturgy, we all have the opportunity to combine tradition and innovation to the degree that is appropriate for each worshipping community.[6] A congregation can look at each part of the liturgy in light of the baptismal themes, values, and seasons and consider ways to incorporate them. There are many ways in each part of the liturgy where we can exercise cautious creativity.

Scripture in the Liturgy

Finding significant pieces of scripture that fit the theme and baptismal vow of the day are great ways of formation for our people, and these pieces of scripture may be incorporated in various sentences throughout the liturgy. This offers one more opportunity for Christian education to be an intimate part of the liturgy, which is Christian formation at its best. Typically, I highlight in bold parts of our regular Sunday readings that the congregation recites as the lector reads the lessons. This reinforces pieces of scripture I want them to learn or pay close attention to on any given Sunday. These same pieces of scripture could be incorporated into a refrain in the Prayers of the People.

Additionally, every liturgy, or maybe only on special occasions, could begin at the font with an opening prayer or words of scripture that reflect baptismal themes or the vow of the season. The procession could begin from there.

Songs of Praise

Episcopalians traditionally sing a special song of praise just after the opening of the service. The BCP provides much flexibility here, for the rubrics make it clear that "another song of praise" can be sung. One that directly relates to the baptismal theme of the season or day could be used. Using a special song for the entire season could provide reinforcement. The Magnificat (BCP, 50), for example, would be appropriate during the season of Advent; the Venite and/or Jubilate (BCP, 44, 82) for the season after Pentecost; Canticle 11 or the Third Song of Isaiah (BCP, 87) for Epiphany season; and "Christ our Passover" (BCP, 83) for Easter season.

---

6. It might do well to remember that most of our traditions were originally innovations that stuck.

Sermons

As discussed in chapter 3, there are many benefits to preaching the theme of each baptismal vow in a season that fits the vow. Sermons could be tailored to "unpack" some of the different meanings of baptism at services where the "Renewal of Vows" is made. This might be appropriate in congregations that renew their vows routinely through the seasons of the year.

Teaching on a theology of baptism during a particular season, special occasion, or recommended Sunday (Easter, Pentecost, All Saints', and the Baptism of Our Lord) would be fruitful:

Advent/Justice: Being a new creation and caring for Creation
Epiphany/Service: Being a child of God, an heir to the throne
Lent/Repentance: Dying with Christ, repentance of sins
Easter/Proclamation: Rising with Christ, forgiveness of sins, being washed clean
Pentecost/Participation: Receiving the Holy Spirit in baptism, being grafted into the Body of Christ

Our Creeds

I know of one congregation that replaces the Nicene Creed with the Renewal of Baptismal Vows every Sunday.[7] A preacher may want to expound on what and how we believe, and how for Christians, praying is believing. The Creed could be followed by a recitation of the baptismal vows, as mentioned earlier, which reinforces our intent for how we live because of what we believe.

The Prayers of the People

The celebrant's "sentence" could set the prayers in the context of the baptismal theme of the day or season. The prayers could be written with that focus in mind and if ministries are being highlighted or commissioned at the service, then some of that group if gifted in this area, could write the prayers. The following is an example of some Prayers of the People to be said during Epiphany season:

7. Devon Anderson sent me an email in 2008 about a parish that does this and it has been quite effective.

We pray for our world leaders. Lord help us to care enough about the world around us to learn the stories of other nations.

We pray for world peace. Lord help us to be people of inner peace and to strive for peace and justice, respecting the dignity of every human being.

We pray for our church leaders. Lord help us to support them by word and action.

We pray for those who are sick and troubled. Lord help us to want to help them.

We pray for our enemies, both political and personal. Lord help us to want to pray for them and help us to love and bless them as you have commanded us to do.

We pray for creation. Lord, in your story of Creation, You have charged each Christian, Jew and Muslim to be stewards of all creation . . . the air we breathe, the sea, the fishes and the animals that creep upon the earth. Help us join hands in caring for all creation.

We pray for the will to stop living lives that consume more of our fair share of the world's resources.

We pray for those who are in danger, sorrow or any kind of trouble. Give us eyes to see the children who grow up in urban war zones, ears to hear their cries and the will to use our power and influence to do something about it.

Confession of Sin

The BCP states that one of the sentences from the Penitential Order (351 or 319) may be used at the confession. A sentence that is written specifically to reinforce the baptismal theme of the day or season may be used. The following is a sample of what some added sentences of confession might sound like during the season of Epiphany:

Dear God, you have chosen us to be a light unto the nations and to proclaim by word and example the good News of God in Christ and yet we continually fail to do so.

We confess that sometimes we contribute more toward the darkness than the light.

We confess our embarrassment at sharing our faith.

We confess our fear of our own abilities to do so and our desire to keep our faith private.

We confess that we are not confident enough about our faith to sometimes even verbalize it.

We confess that we do come too often to your table for solace only, and not for strength.

God forgive us for our fears and give us both the desire and will to follow through on all the promises made in Baptism. **Amen.**

Offertory Sentences

The BCP provides flexibility in what offertory sentences may be said (376 and 343) and even states, "One of the following, or some other appropriate sentence of Scripture, may be used." This would be another opportunity to search for a piece of scripture to exemplify the theme of the day.

For Advent, quotes from the Book of Amos would be appropriate. At dismissal, a preacher might use "Seek good and not evil, that you may live; and so the Lord, the God of hosts will be with you and let justice roll down like waters, and righteousness like an ever flowing stream" (Amos 5:14, 24).

Every Sunday in Epiphany, congregations could read John 13:14–15: "So if I your Lord and teacher, have washed your feet, you also ought to wash one another's feet. For I have set you an example, that you also should do as I as I have done to you."

During Lent, Luke 3:8 could be quoted, especially when John the Baptist proclaims, "Therefore bear fruits worthy of repentance."

The words from Malachi 3:8 could be used by a brave leader of worship during Stewardship Season: "Will anyone rob God? Yet you are robbing me! But you say, 'How are we robbing you?' In your tithes and offerings!"

Micah 6:8 could be used for almost any of the baptismal vows: "He has told you, O mortal, what is good; and what does the Lord require of you but to do justice, and to love kindness and to walk humbly with your God?"

Alms and Oblations

It is quite interesting to note that the rubrics/instructions in the 1979 Book of Common Prayer (333 or 361) require representatives of the congregations to bring forth the offerings of bread and wine, money, or other gifts. Previously the rubrics read, "Deacons, Churchwardens, or other fit persons appointed for that purpose shall bring the offerings to the minister."[8] The rubrics do not use the word "may" here, which is normally used when there is an option of doing or saying what is written. Representatives of a particular ministry that is appropriate for the baptismal theme of the season could bring those forward. They could also bring forward a special gift that relates to their baptismal ministry that would be placed on the altar. Those gifts could be anything from prayer shawls to various sundry articles used in the particular ministry and the members should explain to the congregation the meaning behind the gifts.

It should be noted that, considering the work that Wayne Schwab has done, regarding "members as missionaries," that in congregations where particular families or persons are signed up to bring forth the oblations, they might bring up symbols of their jobs, their schools, or their home life to be blessed. I know of congregations where this has been done at the offertory. I have even heard of a congregation where a policeperson brought up her service weapon to have it blessed that it might never be used.[9] Bringing up oblational items that represent everyday professions or jobs would be especially appropriate during the long season after Pentecost.

The Eucharistic Prayer

On the first Sunday of each new liturgical season, there is an opportunity to use a special Eucharistic Prayer when the baptismal vows are renewed.

---

8. Hatchett, *Commentary*, 348.
9. Holy Trinity Parish, Decatur, Georgia.

A congregation could also use an appropriate Eucharistic Prayer for an entire season that fits the baptismal theme of that season. There are a number of optional Eucharistic Prayers in the BCP and in *Enriching Our Worship*. Eucharistic Prayers C and D probably make the most sense for baptisms.

In congregations that do not use Prayer C (BCP, 369–372) very often, just being different can be effective. Prayer C also rehearses our history with more detail. Considering the baptismal promises, it spells out that we come not for solace only, but for strength [to carry out our vows?], not for pardon only, but for renewal [to carry out our vows?]. The words, "Let the grace of this Holy Communion make us one body, one spirit in Christ," echo the beginning of a service for baptism. There is a specific reference to water and spirit in the words, " . . . and made a new people by water and the Spirit." Eucharistic Prayer D (BCP, 372–376) has the advantage of incorporating the Prayers of the People, so prayers for the world and wider church can be added, since the Prayers for the Candidates usually replace the Prayers of the People in the service for Holy Baptism.

The Dismissal

This of all times and places in the liturgy is to remind the people of the theme of the day's sermon, and so adding to the dismissal would be a positive reinforcement. The words and purposes of the dismissal have changed throughout the generations.[10] A congregation that is modeled after baptismal values might choose to quote various scriptures that relate to the vow of the season.

Advent

Deacon   Hear the words of the prophet Micah:
He has told you O mortal, what is good; and what does the Lord require of you but to do justice, and to love kindness, and to walk humbly with your God?

Micah 6:8

---

10. Hatchett, *Commentary*, 396.

Now go in peace to love and serve the Lord.

Epiphany

Deacon Listen to these words from the book of James!

What good is it, my brothers and sisters, if you say you have faith but do not have works? Can faith save you? If a brother or sister is naked and lacks daily food and one of you say to them, "Go in peace; keep warm and eat your fill," and yet you do not supply their bodily needs, what is the good of that?

James 2:14–17

Deacon Now let us go forth into the world showing forth our faith, not only with our lips but with our lives!

People **Thanks be to God.**

Easter

Deacon Listen to the words from the Gospel of Matthew!

And Jesus came and said to them, "Go therefore and make disciples of all nations, baptizing them in the name of the Father and the Son and the Holy Spirit, and teaching them to obey everything I have commanded you. And remember, I am with you always, to the end of the age."

Matthew 28:18–20

Deacon Let us go forth in the name of Christ! Alleluia! Alleluia! Alleluia!

People **Thanks be to God. Alleluia! Alleluia! Alleluia!**[11]

Pentecost

Deacon Listen to the words of the prophet Joel!

In the last days it will be, God declares, that I will pour out my spirit upon all flesh. Then everyone who calls upon the name of the Lord shall be saved.

Joel 2:28–32

---

11. Many liturgical reforms have come from the practice of the people and the people throughout the country have begun adding extra "Alleluias" to the dismissal, and I have no doubt that this custom will be incorporated into any future liturgical revisions.

Deacon	Let us go forth into the world rejoicing in the power of the Spirit.
People	**Thanks be to God**

Special Liturgies

Congregations who focus upon baptism may begin to expect direct references to the baptismal covenant in other liturgies. This can also be a method for leading congregations toward "living into their baptism."* I have been surprised, having immersed myself in these baptismal values, when at ordinations and funerals there were no direct references to the baptismal covenant, especially since those services reflect baptismal values. It is not that the BCP spells out the reasons for them to have direct references, but having studied them so much myself, I expect them now. Possible examples that flow out of my own imagination are included below. Something similar might be done at consecrations of buildings, celebrations of new ministry, and the many other special services that are provided for in the Book of Common Prayer, *The Book of Occasional Services,* and supplemental liturgical resources for other denominations. Those who plan liturgies will need to explore how to incorporate baptismal imagery into their special liturgies until eventually it will come to them naturally.

Funerals and Weddings

Funeral services remind us that we have died with Christ and will rise with him. We could begin with a prayer at the font, as I have seen done at Roman Catholic funerals, including sprinkling the coffin with baptismal waters at the beginning. The priest says something like:

> *Grant that all who have been baptized into Christ's death and resurrection may die to sin and rise to newness of life, and that through the grave and gate of death we may pass with him to our joyful resurrection. AMEN.*[12]

If a congregation is used to reaffirming their baptismal vows on a regular basis, then reaffirming these vows after the homily might be

---

12. This prayer is included in the prayers of the Rite I funeral service on page 480. There is no reason not to pray it as the coffin is sprinkled with water.

an appropriate time. It could be introduced with something like the following:

Our brother/sister was washed in Baptism and anointed with the Holy Spirit. Through the Paschal mystery, dear friends, we are buried with Christ by Baptism into his death and raised with him to newness of life. Please turn to page 292 in The Book of Common Prayer and let us join in fellowship with N. and all the saints and renew our own baptismal covenant. Do you reaffirm . . .

During wedding services we are reminded of the third vow, for Paul says that marriage is a symbol of Christ's love for the church, and therefore marriage is a living proclamation. A wedding could begin at the font with a prayer such as:

We have all been made one in Christ through the waters of Baptism. N and N now come to be made one in the sacrament of marriage. Please turn to page 292 in The Book of Common Prayer and let us join in fellowship with them and all the saints and renew our own baptismal covenant. Do you reaffirm . . .

Ordinations

Ordination services *should* include the renewal of our baptismal vows! Setting aside a person for holy orders is a good and joyful time to remind ourselves that we all share in "the priesthood of all believers" and in the ordained ministry. A candidate for bishop could reaffirm the Baptismal Covenant with the entire congregation before being consecrated a bishop.

Blessing the Oil

The *Services for Trial Use*[13] for The Episcopal Church from the 1970s suggested that the bishop bless the oil for chrism in front of the congregation. Some bishops (in denominations that have bishops) may want to consider changing the recent custom of having the blessing of the oil with a

---

13. These pamphlets were published in the 1960s and 1970s when The Episcopal Church was exploring new rites for the 1979 prayer book.

gathering of clergy only.[14] Congregations can be encouraged to have the oil blessed on the bishop's regular visit even if there are no baptisms, and it might be a good thing to store blessed oil in a cruet large enough to be visible to the congregation year-round, or at least during baptisms. This too was suggested in the proposed Rite of Baptism offered in *Prayer Book Studies XVIII* in the "Additional Directions and Suggestions" section (42): "The blessing of the chrism is reserved to the bishop alone. It is desirable that this be done in the presence of the congregation. Oil for this purpose is left in the church to be used by the priest when the bishop is not present."[15]

The consecration of chrism, as noted earlier, often tends to be neglected in action, instruction, preaching, and placement, and that is why there is a lengthy discussion of it here. Marion Hatchett reinforces this in saying, "The chrism is to be consecrated at the time of the bishop's visitation and in sight of the people. Its use on baptismal occasions, in addition to the time of the bishop's visitation (in addition to other significations vividly symbolizes the connection between baptism and the bishop)."[16]

Ruth Meyers makes this clear in her review of the use of chrism in *Praying Shapes Believing*, and reminds us of Jim Turrell's suggestion in his book *Celebrating the Rites of Initiation*, that not only should the anointing take place where all can see the act, but an abundance of fragrant oil should be used so the congregation can see the oil and smell it.[17] When the bishop is not present, this prayer can still be offered while omitting the words, "We pray you to consecrate this oil."

We can offer proclamation around the Chrism of Oil. Too often the anointing is hidden from the congregation, and they have little idea of what is happening. Preaching on this to a congregation the Sunday before the baptism or just before the baptism is teaching about baptism.

---

14. *Services for Trial Use: Authorized Alternatives to Prayer Book Service* (New York: Church Hymnal Corporation 1971), 22, 28.

15. The SLC, *Prayer Book Studies XVIII on Baptism and Confirmation* (New York: Church Pension Fund, 1970), 43.

16. Marion J. Hatchett, *Commentary on the American Prayer Book* (San Francisco: Harper Collins, 1980), 276.

17. Ruth Meyers and Leonel Mitchell, *Praying Shapes Believing, A Theological Commentary on The Book of Common Prayer* (New York: Seabury Press, 2016), 121–124.

Anointing of priests and kings and of early church catechumens—those preparing for baptism—is an ancient tradition, not to mention that the Messiah is translated as "the anointed one." Anointing for exorcism and chrismation—anointing with oil—of the newly baptized were part of ancient Christian traditions. Lee Mitchell notes that anointing with oil was part and parcel of bathing in the ancient secular world, and that anointing in religious ceremonies was part of the Roman and Jewish traditions, not to mention the anointing of kings. Infants baptized in some Orthodox traditions are completely anointed with oil.

Christians saw Jesus as *Rex Unctus*, the anointed king, and that is traced back to the Hebrew scriptures. Many Christian traditions associated the anointing with the Holy Spirit and with bishops. Much oil was used, whether anointing the whole body or the forehead. This was all part of one whole rite of initiation (washing, anointing, and laying on of hands), and confirmation came later, so the 1979 BCP "put it back together" again.[18] Mitchell concludes in 1966:

> Those which have separated Baptism and Confirmation have lost their hold on the unity of the rite and thereby introduced manifold theological and pastoral problems.... In any restoration of the rite of Christian initiation to its primitive integrity, the anointing with chrism should take its place with the washing in water, the signing of the cross [making the sign of the cross], the laying on of hands, and the reception of the Eucharist as one of the rites by which we become members of the mystical Body of Christ.[19]

It is clear from the BCP 1979 that Mitchell's opinion was heeded. (He did after all participate in the revisions of the initiation rite for the BCP.) Anointing had been included in Thomas Cranmer's first prayer book, but then taken out of the rest of the versions.[20] After "intelligent research" the reformers decided to once again incorporate the anointing into the baptismal rite.[21]

---

18. Leonel L. Mitchell, *Baptismal Anointing* (London, SPCK, 1966), 172–175.

19. Mitchell, 172–175.

20. Thomas Cranmer created the first prayer book for the Church of England after it broke away from Rome.

21. Marion J. Hatchett, *Commentary on the American Prayer Book* (San Francisco: Harper Collins, 1980), 275–276.

The Role of Bishops in Confirmation and Baptism

The 1979 Book of Common Prayer was greatly influenced by William Palmer Ladd and Massey Shepherd,[22] who believed strongly that baptism should be full initiation into the church. Shepherd stated that there are four holy orders, and since baptism is every Christian's entrance into Holy Orders, confirmation was redundant.[23]

> Indeed I should go so far as to say that there is more meaning in the Episcopal office [the diocesan bishop] succeeding from the apostles when it is viewed as a mission to preach and baptize than when it is restricted to a duty to visit and confirm ... The first step in the reconstruction of the initiation liturgy would seem to me one that "restores" to the bishop *his/her* [my updated language] presidency and office in TOTAL initiation of the Christian and not just in that part we call Confirmation.[24]

Aidan Kavanagh expands on this idea of baptism as the "first step," noting, "there is no other time of year, with the possible exception of the visitation of the bishop, which so remarkably fits the setting of Christian initiation."[25] Baptism is where everything begins.

It will take many actions around the baptismal journey to speed up how quickly baptismal values are instilled in all of us, and that is why some of this should be done with and through our regional and national church leaders, regardless of the denomination. Bishops have had primary roles in the churches of the past. It was the bishop who baptized and was the primary teacher in early churches. We are baptized into the "Church universal" and the bishop represents that connection. In this age when churches think and act so congregationally, it might be good to connect baptism and bishops.

Many early churches understood Jesus's commission to go into the world baptizing in the name of the Father, Son, and Holy Spirit, as a commission to the apostles (bishops). Leonel Mitchell, in his memoir, notes that those who revised this rite of initiation wanted to place the bishop

22. Massey H. Shepherd, *Liturgy and Education* (New York: Seabury, 1965), 106.
23. Shepherd, *Liturgy and Education*, 106.
24. Shepherd, *Liturgy and Education*, 106.
25. Chapman, "Eight Faces," 9.

at the center of the baptism service,[26] which of course would mean that the newly baptized who were anointed by the bishop would be fully initiated into the church, and that a future rite of confirmation, as it had been understood, would not be necessary. The 1991 Fourth International Anglican Liturgical Consultation at Toronto in its *Principles of Christian Initiation* recommended that "the pastoral rite of confirmation be delegated by the bishop to a presbyter."[27]

> The laity functions as the fundamental Holy Order in the Church, and all of us are made laymen [archaic language] in our Baptism. We must rid ourselves of all the common parlance that suggest that Confirmation is the so-called 'ordination of the laity'. Baptism is the layman's ordination.[28]

Many denominations are struggling with what to do with the rite of confirmation. Roman Catholic bishops can authorize priests to perform confirmation on Holy Saturday. In some of the trial liturgies for creating a new prayer book in The Episcopal Church, the rubrics stated that the priest, in the absence of the bishop, was to lay hands upon confirmands,[29] yet the rubrics from that same service repeatedly stated that the bishop was expected to be present for baptisms.[30]

A powerful way to accomplish part of the purposes of this book would be for bishops, General Convention, and dioceses to agree with the specific rubrics of the Book of Common Prayer stating that baptisms are usually presided over by the bishop. Imagine convocational or diocesan baptisms instead of diocesan confirmations. These would give cause for even greater festive liturgies, and reinforce the importance and the sense of unity around baptism. One Spirit, one Faith, one Baptism, one Bishop. Local clergy could still do the actual baptism, while the

---

26. Leonel Mitchell, a draft memoir emailed to the author in 2009.

27. Meyers, *Continuing the Reformation*, 269–270.

28. Massey H. Shepherd, *Liturgy and Education* (New York: Seabury, 1965), 106.

29. I was at a baptism recently where the bishop was present, yet the priest did the baptism (which would be expected) and the anointing with oil and the laying on of hands, as the bishop stood by. I am assuming this was done without either the priest or bishop noting that the bishop should have been the one to do the anointing and laying on of hands, according to the rubrics of the BCP.

30. *Authorized Services, 1973* (New York: Church Hymnal Corporation, 1973), 29.

bishop could preside and perform the anointing with oil and laying on of hands.[31]

The bishops often want to hold onto doing the confirmations at a later time, so maybe a diocese gets their feet wet by offering a diocesan baptism every All Saints' Day. This could also be when clergy reaffirm their vows. Either way, having diocesan and/or convocational baptisms, either occasionally or regularly with the bishop presiding, could be one large step for increasing the perceived importance of the unity of baptism and the Baptismal Covenant. Bishops could at least add their wax seals from their rings to baptismal certificates. The bishop has been willing to add their wax seal to our baptismal certificates at my current church.

Naturally, some congregations may never experience a service with all "orders" (bishops, priests, deacons, and laypeople) present. During the ordination service of a bishop may be a good time for all priests and deacons to renew their ordination vows, especially since they derive their ordained ministry from both their bishop and the people of God.[32] It is powerful and meaningful to hear where, when, and by whom the candidate had been ordained deacon and priest. How much more meaningful to all those (the baptized) present to hear where, when, and by whom the candidate was baptized (and confirmed).

The Episcopal prayer book also contains some dissonance regarding bishops and baptism. The BCP makes explicit in the service for new ministry that the bishop is the primary person to preside at baptisms. In the Introduction on page 561, the bishop hands the priest a vessel of water and says, "*N.*, take this water, and help me [help the bishop] baptize in obedience to our Lord." However, there is no specific reference to a bishop's call to baptize in the service for the Ordination of a Bishop (BCP, 511–524) nor in the additional directions on page 552.[33]

---

31. This addresses the current debate in the House of Bishops over their role in confirmation, in that being a crucial person at baptisms would make being "needed" or "valued" at confirmations redundant. See footnotes 43 and 45.

32. See pages 526, 532, and 538, 543 of the BCP regarding the duties of priest and deacons as they relate to their relationship with the bishop, other ordained ministers, and the people. Doing this with each new bishop could be an appropriate reminder to our clergy in light of the instances of clergy disavowing their bishops.

33. The only time in the service that even a form of the word "baptism" appears occurs during the Examination when the candidate is asked, "Will you encourage and support all *baptized* people in their gifts and ministries. . . .." On the other hand, the BCP does make it clear

Mention is made of preaching and teaching in the preface for Apostles and Ordination on page 381, but no specific mention of baptizing and training disciples. There is mention of being responsible for the administration (in general) of all the sacraments, but even then, it goes on to spell out the bishop's responsibility for ordaining priests and deacons, which are only a couple of the sacraments. *After having immersed myself in the baptismal imagery in the Book of Common Prayer, there appears to me to be a loud silence on baptism when we ordain the person who is primarily responsible for baptisms.* This dissonance could be addressed in some or all of the following suggestions for the liturgy for the ordination of bishops:

1. Replace the Nicene Creed in the bishop ordination service with the renewal of baptismal vows, rephrasing the statement by the presiding bishop on page 519 to read:

   N., through these promises you have committed yourself to God to serve all the baptized in the office of bishop. We therefore call upon you, chosen to be a guardian of the Church's faith, to lead all of us in the renewal of our baptismal vows.

2. Add the words "to baptize" to the preface for Apostles and Ordinations.

3. Substitute "Holy Communion and Holy Baptism" for the words "New Covenant" in the second paragraph of the Examination.[34]

4. Publicly certify where, when, and by whom the candidate had been baptized.[35]

5. Print somewhere in the bulletin the part of the catechism entitled "The Ministry" to remind all the orders gathered for this event of their own ministries (BCP, 855–856).

---

during the Examination at the ordinations of priests that they are to "...share in the administration of Holy Baptism."

34. Why not spell it out since many attendees to the ordination may not know that the sacraments of the New Covenant are Holy Communion and Holy Baptism. (I am assuming since the BCP speaks of ordaining priests and deacons immediately after speaking of the sacraments of the New Covenant, that ordinations and the other "minor sacraments" were not included.)

35. I attended an ordination of a bishop and credentials verifying that the person had previously been ordained deacon and priest were formally presented, yet no certification of baptism was presented.

6. Remind all present that baptism is ordination for ministry, the "priesthood of all believers" (the Protestant concept that all the baptized have the responsibility of priests).

The ordination of a new bishop is the beginning of a new relationship and a new start for a diocese. What better time for the whole people of God gathered with all orders present to renew the baptismal vows that all orders share!

I mention all of this to emphasize that the active support by bishops, dioceses and General Convention is key to baptismal values being incorporated by congregations. *It works both ways.* Incorporating the bishop's role in baptism and the renewing of our baptismal vows during an ordination of a bishop may be one of the many liturgical preludes needed to lead all of us deeper into the call of our baptism. What a bishop or regional authority says and does *is* important and *adds* importance. Bishops could be the cornerstone for encouraging congregations to renew the Baptismal Covenant year-round and for encouraging congregations, dioceses, and the national church to structure themselves upon a baptismal ecclesiology.

Questions for Reflection

1. Imagine diocesan baptisms and allowing priests to confirm—how would your congregation respond?

2. Are there special liturgies not mentioned that you think would be a good time to renew the baptismal vows?

CHAPTER 6

The Service of Holy Baptism

Preaching Perspectives from the Service of Holy Baptism

The heart of the rite of baptism is the service of Holy Baptism, which either directly professes or indirectly alludes to the full variety of baptismal actions, theologies, and implications invoked by the services' words and rituals. These words and actions, found on pages 297–314 of the BCP, declare a plain truth and yet still give us cause us to meditate on them, as well as to wonder and preach about them. They address the theological underpinnings of baptism within almost any denomination. This chapter will focus on specific passages from the service of Holy Baptism itself.

The service taps into Paul's use of baptism as an opportunity to preach about other theologies, and the importance of Paul's emphasis on what we believe and how we behave in the context of baptism. Here is what Paul says regarding one faith and one baptism in Ephesians:

> I therefore, the prisoner in the Lord, beg you to lead a life worthy of the calling to which you have been called, with all humility and gentleness, with patience, bearing with one another in love, making every effort to maintain the unity of the Spirit in the bond of peace. *There is one body and one Spirit, just as you were called to the one hope of your calling, one Lord, one faith, one baptism, one God and Father of all,* who is above all and through all and in all. [emphasis mine]
>
> *Ephesians 4:1–6*

The Book of Common Prayer paraphrases this piece from Ephesians to begin the service for Holy Baptism on page 299. Paul's appeal for unity in baptism echoes his appeal for unity in Jesus Christ, as one body with many parts. We might do well to sometimes follow his example. Early

Christians saw those to be baptized go down under the water and rise up. They saw the white robes "put on." Paul used this baptismal imagery to speak to what it means to experience the death of the old self and birth of a new self, to "put on" Christ and to urge his people to live lives worthy of new life.

Paul describes that experience as he speaks of dying and rising with Christ. Does this dying and rising with Christ actually happen in the act of baptism, or does Paul use the act of baptism to describe the experience and/or remind people of the experience of many Christians? To quote a former professor whose name I cannot remember, Paul simply says over and over again in so many ways, "Remember your baptism!"

During the Thanksgiving over the Water, many Christians recite, "Through the [water] we are reborn by the Holy Spirit" (BCP, 306). What does it mean to be reborn by the Holy Spirit? Is this the charismatic experience of the apostles at Pentecost; or of the gentiles in Cornelius's household to whom Peter preached; or through the laying on of Paul's hands on some disciples who (apparently to Paul) had not received the Holy Spirit in their baptism; or is it the transforming experience of Dennis Bennett, an Episcopal priest, and the many who experienced the charismatic renewal in the 1970s?

John 3:16 speaks of being born of the Spirit and water. Is this a theological concept to be lifted up at baptisms? Once again, the ritual reflects rebirth, a reality that many, though not all Christians, have experienced. Baptism can reflect what has happened, what is happening, and/or what is yet to come. It can be a calling to a future experience, reflecting a deeper unseen reality that the church declares at baptism.

> *"That those who here are cleansed from sin and born again may continue forever in the risen life of Jesus Christ." (BCP, 307)*

Are we cleansed from sin momentarily, or is there an eternal change of who we are in this world and the world to come? What if the newly baptized did not mean it, or was living in notorious sin? What if the minister did not mean it? Are those sins wiped away at baptism? Are we wiped clean of original sin? What is the risen life in Christ, and what is the ongoing experience of that for members of a congregation? Is it a current reality in the rite, or is it a calling, as Paul would say, to live the life we were intended and raised to live? Is it a "recalling" of what has already happened? Theologians and church officials have answered those questions down through the ages, in a variety of ways and in ways that contradict one another.

Looking at the sacrament itself, Augustine gives a starting point to understanding the power of the spoken ritual:

> The word is joined to the water and the result is a sacrament, itself becoming in a sense, a visible word as well . . . . Whence the power of water is exalted as to bathe the body and cleanse the soul, if it is not through the action of the word; not because it is spoken but because it is believed.[1]

Augustine reveals a gravitational pull between the act, the medium, the words, and belief—and in that tension, we discover sacraments, "outward and visible signs of inward and spiritual grace, given by Christ as sure and certain means by which we receive that grace" (The Catechism, BCP, 857).

"Holy Baptism is full initiation by water and the Holy Spirit into Christ's Body the Church." (BCP, 298)

What does it mean to be a full member of the Body of Christ? Speaking pastorally, the preacher may want to preach about all God's children coming to the communion table, not for a blessing from the priest but to receive the body and blood of Christ. There are still many parents who will not let their children receive communion before they are confirmed, even though they are baptized. This is an opportunity to preach about the direct connection between baptism and Holy Communion. A preacher may contemplate what they would want parents to know about baptism and prepare to instruct the entire congregation in that vein.

The service In the prayer book makes clear that we are baptized into the whole Body of Christ, and the preacher who is preaching to some congregants from other denominations may want to take an opportunity to note that no one is baptized an Episcopalian, or a Presbyterian, or a Roman Catholic, or a Methodist, but as a Christian. (This is also a good time to remind them it is the Lord's Supper, not a particular denomination's

---

1. Maxwell Johnson, ed., *Sacraments and Worship, the Sources of Christian Theology* (Louisville, KY: Westminster John Knox Press, 2012), 2.

Supper.) The point is that we are grafted into the one Body of Christ, and baptism, if not the cause of this unification, is foremost a symbol and reminder that the grafting has happened, creating eternal bonds. This could be a theme for preaching baptism on All Saints' Day.

"You are sealed by the Holy Spirit in baptism and marked as Christ own for ever." (BCP, 308)

What is it about "forever" that people often do not get? Doubts about the indissolubility of baptism come up regularly in counseling sessions and in comments to ministers and preachers, especially by people who have been brought up in other faith traditions. What is often read at funerals from Romans 8, reflects the reality that nothing can separate us from the love of God in Christ Jesus, neither height nor depth, nor principalities nor powers, neither life nor death … which can just as well mean today, neither doubt nor faith, neither church attendance, nor absence, neither behaving badly nor doing good works, nor marital status or gender, nor baptism nor the absence of baptism, and so on. Teaching that baptism is for all eternity may help the newly baptized have a sense of assurance as they begin their journey, and help those who have been baptized for some time to have patience in their ongoing baptismal journey.

"Confess the faith of Christ crucified, proclaim his resurrection, and share with us in his eternal priesthood." (BCP, 308)

Now is the time for the newly baptized—and all the baptized—to be able to share in the experience of faith. We are the royal and eternal priesthood of believers after all! All the baptized are ordained in baptism and set aside for the ministry of proclamation, blessing, healing, and reconciliation.

Scripture itself tells how the Spirit moves in a way that institutions cannot control. Sometimes the Spirit falls during baptism and sometimes the Spirit falls before baptism. Paul discovers a group of disciples who had been baptized but have not received or even heard of the Holy Spirit (Acts 19:1–7). The Ethiopian says to Philip in Acts 8, "Here is some water. What is to prevent me from being baptized?" No great training or education takes place. The criminal on the cross was "saved" without baptism (Acts 23:43). Martyrs who were in training for baptism and not yet baptized were considered baptized in their own blood. There is little training or formation for anyone baptized in the New Testament stories. Catechesis—the formation of disciples—more often than not came after baptism, such as in Paul's case (Acts 9).

It is in light of mystery that we reflect upon the theologies of baptism expressed in scripture and by numerous theologians within Christendom, recognizing that Christendom has rarely agreed upon what baptism is or what happens in it—and probably never will. It is amazing how so many theologians have sharply disagreed on theology and ecclesiology with such a sense of clarity, as though they knew the truth, the whole truth, and nothing but the truth. History has shown repeatedly how wrong were those who were so sure they were right. Theologians would do well to preface their remarks with Paul's words, "We [see/view/do/teach/profess theology and liturgy] through a glass darkly."

The service of Holy Baptism covers the primary theological bases and experiences of baptism and recalls the work of Christ in us, through us, before us, and after us. The rite of baptism is as much, if not more, for the congregation as it is for the ones being baptized, for we need constant reminders. Therefore, continued preaching and teaching on baptism and renewing the Covenant must remain a critical goal for the church.

A Template for a Service of Holy Baptism

Preachers should work to incorporate many of the ideas already mentioned, but if the actual Baptism is not a "pull out all the stops" beautiful and extravagant experience, then all the above is just loud noise. The great drama is more to remind attending parishioners of their own baptisms—the journey and the implications for living—than to instruct the ones being baptized. *This is why I do not require intense baptism classes for the parents or sponsors—because if we are doing liturgy well, then over time all will be educated about baptism.* Remember that neither Peter on the Day of Pentecost, nor Philip with the Ethiopian eunuch, required any intense catechumenate or training program!

Those who revised the rites of initiation in liturgical denominations wanted to lift up the ministry of *all* the baptized, recognizing that baptism is not only a consecration of our selves, our souls, and our bodies, but a type of ordination and commission for ministry. The Eucharist, the catechism, and the rubrics throughout prayer books all support this.

However, as already mentioned, there is currently some misunderstanding regarding the priority of the ministry of the baptized and the ministry of the ordained. Ruth Meyers in her booklet *Baptism and Ministry, Liturgical Studies One*, quotes William Seth Adams in this regard:

> William Seth Adams argues the case for an ecclesiology built on a "baptismal paradigm." Adams is critical of the church's current practice of ordination rites that overshadows the baptismal rite and argues effectively for a reformation of practice that would put baptism in its appropriate position of primacy.[2]

Comparing what is involved for baptisms with what is involved in ordinations, confirmations, and weddings may shed some light on the fact that many opportunities for formation might be missing from the way we currently engage baptisms, and give us some ideas on how we can further enhance baptism. The non-verbal signals to parishioners often communicate that baptisms are not as important as ordinations or confirmations. Let's compare some of these practices, remembering that there are many exceptions to these examples:

Weddings

Invitations are sent to the church community for weddings. The church is cleaned up, special bulletins with the entire service are printed, and other extraordinary preparations are made. Contrast this with baptisms, where invitations are rarely sent; too often the church community is not informed of a baptism ahead of time; special bulletins are rarely printed; and the church facilities rarely are cleaned up in anticipation of a baptism.

Ordinations

Approval from the vestry or board is required at every step toward ordination. However, too often the leadership may not even know there is a baptism coming up. Leadership and members of the church may not even know the name of the person to be baptized.

Those to be ordained are required to sign a statement of belief about Holy Scriptures in front of the entire congregation, whereas the newly

---

2. Meyers, ed., *Baptism and Ministry*, 44.

baptized and their sponsors are not required to sign anything. Maybe the candidates for baptism or their sponsors could sign a copy of the Baptismal Covenant along with witnesses.

Confirmations

Bishops and/or regional heads are present for ordinations and confirmations, but rarely if ever present for baptisms. The bishop signs confirmation and ordination certificates but does not sign baptism certificates. Sometimes there is one combined service when the bishop comes, yet rarely does the idea occur to people to combine services for baptisms.

There is usually an elaborate reception for the newly ordained, married, or confirmed; whereas the reception for the newly baptized, if there is one, is often small[3] and the church usually makes a bigger deal about the rite of confirmation.

Holy Baptism Rubrics with Commentary

One way or another, if we are to raise the expectations of the liturgy for baptism then we will need to treat it with great expectations and celebrations. Ways to do this are addressed in detail below. The basic service is taken directly from the Book of Common Prayer, pages 299—314. Most of the enhancements have been taken from other services and from collects and prayers from other parts of the BCP. Some ideas for the service have been borrowed from alternative prayer books from The Church of England, Canada, and New Zealand.

Rubrics are a crucial element to understanding the liturgy and moving through the liturgy, though they often go unnoticed. The Church of England's alternative prayer book, *Common Worship*, uses rubrics much more than the BCP does, and it includes quite a bit of practical instruction in the body of the liturgy—much like the old 1928 Episcopal prayer book did. Some new rubrics have been added to this sample liturgy, and sometimes they are clarified or expanded so the people do not miss the point. Each will be explained as we work our way through the liturgy.

---

3. My experience is that the more elaborate reception is often held at the parents' home, which has echoes of the old habit of private baptisms.

Suggestions for the use of voice and tone in the service are included. Preaching happens even in the tone of one's voice. Preachers and other religious speakers can be more intentional about *how* they say *what* they say, especially considering the magnitude of what they are doing, which is incorporating a person into the kingdom of God. Being conscious of tone, word, and deed can impact how people respond and absorb the importance of the service. The ministers should consider setting the example if they are not already using tones to emphasize aspects of any liturgy. However, they can and will respond to the enthusiasm of the celebrant, and rubrics will not only help them understand where we are headed but encourage them to respond with appropriate feeling.

This template is not intended to be used in its entirety but is presented to provide inspiration for those who plan baptismal services. They will want to pick and choose which parts they would incorporate into their own services.[4] All these methods can reinforce one another and indeed build upon the other. In Episcopal terms, it is not either/or, but both/and, or as I like to say of the Episcopal way, "*many/plus*"!

Here we will explore ways to liturgically proclaim, enhance, and support the values of baptism at actual baptism services, including how we prepare for and engage with them. I have used The Episcopal Church's BCP as a template but have included parts from Anglican and other denominations' rites of baptism. Enhancing the service for Holy Baptism goes hand in hand with promoting the symbols and values of baptism routinely, for expanding the actual service will naturally flow from a congregation that values the symbols and meanings of baptism and who has heard baptismal values routinely preached. The reverse may be true as well. If congregations pull out all the stops for actual baptismal services, they might be more open to exploring more prominent font locations or reciting baptismal vows on Sundays when there are no baptisms.

Concerning the Service

Holy Baptism is full initiation by water and the Holy Spirit into Christ's Body the Church. The bond which God establishes in Baptism is indissoluble.

---

4. Congregations are often resistant to any changes in the liturgy and there may be less resistance to liturgical changes that are made at baptisms and other special services if they have come to value baptism.

Holy Baptism is appropriately administered within the Eucharist as the chief service on a Sunday or other feast.

The bishop, when present, is the celebrant; and is expected to preach the Word and preside at Baptism and the Eucharist. At Baptism, the bishop officiates at the Presentation and Examination of Candidates; says the Thanksgiving over the Water; [consecrates[5] the oil of chrism;] reads the prayer, "Heavenly Father, we thank you that by water and the Holy Spirit . . . ;" and officiates at what follows.

In the absence of a bishop, a priest is the celebrant and presides at the service. If a priest uses chrism of oil in signing the newly baptized, it must have been previously consecrated by the bishop.

Each candidate for Holy Baptism is to be sponsored by one or more baptized persons.

Sponsors of adults and older children present their candidates and thereby signify their endorsement of the candidates and their intention to support them by prayer and example in their Christian life. Sponsors of infants, commonly called godparents, present their candidates, make promises in their own names, and also take vows on behalf of their candidates.

It is fitting that parents be included among the godparents of their own children. Parents and godparents are to be instructed in the meaning of Baptism, in their duties to help the new Christians grow in the knowledge and love of God, and in their responsibilities as members of his Church. (BCP, 298)

Commentary

Remember—rubrics preach! The intention with these initial rubrics is to communicate how important this event is in the life of the parish. Combining multiple services into one is appropriate when possible, which can symbolize one faith, one baptism, and one hope for all.

It is recommended the entire service be printed in a bulletin because it is a special day and so visitors will better be able to engage the liturgy.

---

5. I have added this because as *The Book of Occasional Services* recommends, bishops should always bless the oil of chrism on their normal visits to the congregations.

Greeters may welcome members of the congregation by offering them an empty water bottle. They will be invited to fill these bottles from the font after the service so they can take them home.

The bishop, if present, is the chief celebrant. The chancel party, baptismal party, and other representatives of ministries in the parish gather near the font. The font is censed if using incense is customary. If there are adult catechumens, it is expected that the various ceremonies for catechumens, as found in *The Book of Occasional Services*, have been previously observed.

The "Additional Directions," on page 312 of the BCP, provide that when a bishop is present, or *on other occasions for sufficient reason* [my italics], the Collect and one or more of the Lessons provided for use at baptism (see pages 203, 254, and 928 of the BCP) may be substituted for the Proper of the Day. Baptism could constitute "sufficient reason" for setting aside the Collect of the Day and the readings appointed for the day and replacing them with the Collect for baptism and the readings set aside for baptism.[6] Using the same readings for every baptism might help set this service apart, and people may remember the readings if there are enough baptisms. The preacher can preach variations on the readings.

Beginning the service of Holy Baptism in a unique manner will set it apart, begging the question of all participants, "Why is this service different from any other service?" It is hoped that this kind of question, the sort that comes from the youngest child at the Jewish Passover Feast, the original Paschal Feast, will stir up the imagination with suggestions. Banners, dancers, and kites enhance the festive nature of this service. After all, how exciting should it be that we welcome a new child of God into the kingdom of God?

The Service for Holy Baptism

The Call

(adapted from *Common Worship*, used in The Church of England, the marriage ceremony, and with some of my own insertions)

---

6. If a bishop's permission is needed, it would be wise to get it, since the for some denominations it is stated that "at the principal service on Sunday or other feast, the Collect and Lessons are properly those of the Day."

Celebrant

Dear friends in Christ, we love because God first loves us. In Baptism God declares that love; in Christ, God calls us to respond.

Baptism is the beginning of the journey of faith. Each of us is at a different point in that journey and today, we journey with those who come to be baptized.

The bond which God establishes in Holy Baptism is an indissoluble one and Holy Baptism is full initiation into Christ's Body, the Church, by water and the Holy Spirit and the laying on of hands.

Those who are baptized are cleansed from sin and born again. Through the Paschal mystery, dear friends, we are buried with Christ in the waters of Baptism and raised with him to newness of life. We are sealed by the Holy Spirit and marked as Christ's own forever!

Let us pray for those who are about to enter into this holy mystery.

Silence

O God, you prepared your disciples for the coming of the Spirit through the teaching of your Son Jesus Christ; make the hearts and minds of your servants ready to receive the blessing of the Holy Spirit that they may be filled with the strength of his presence; through Jesus Christ our Lord.[7]

AMEN.

Commentary

The Call and the Exhortation (the Exhortation is optional at a later point in the service) is a sermon unto itself, and calls to mind our history of baptism and various theologies of baptism. This section is called "The Call" in the *New Zealand Prayer Book,* and called "The Pastoral Introduction" in the alternative prayer books for Canada and The Church of England. The purpose here is to include some of the basic information that is already

---

7. Prayer 15, "For those about to be baptized or to renew their Baptismal Covenant," BCP, 819.

referred to in the instructions for baptism on pages 298 and 312–313 of the BCP. This idea comes from *Common Worship*, an alternative prayer book for The Church of England, where the minister reads these rubrics and pieces of information at the beginning of the service.

This "Call" may be done from the font and the Prayer of Thanksgiving and blessing over the water could be said. A bowl may be used and brought to the front for the actual baptism so everyone can see. It is also a good time to splash the people while bringing the bowl forward. The concept of "Exhortation" has historical precedent, according to Marion Hatchett, and is also supported in some of the original trial liturgies of the American prayer books from the '60s and '70s.[8] We do this in the Ash Wednesday liturgy as well.[9]

Thanksgiving Over the Water

(adapted from BCP, 306)

The Celebrant blesses the water, first saying

	The Lord be with you.
People	And also with you.
Celebrant	Let us give thanks to the Lord our God.
People	It is right to give him thanks and praise.

Celebrant

We thank you, Almighty God, for the gift of water.
Over it the Holy Spirit moved in the beginning of creation.
Through it you led the children of Israel out of their bondage in Egypt into the land of promise. In it your Son Jesus received the baptism of John and was anointed by the Holy Spirit as the Messiah, the Christ, to lead us, through his death and resurrection, from the bondage of sin into everlasting life.

We thank you, Father, for the water of Baptism. In it we are buried with Christ in his death. By it we share in his resurrection. Through it we are reborn by the Holy Spirit. Therefore in joyful obedience to your Son, we

---

8. Hatchett, *Commentary*, 260.
9. *BCP*, 264–265.

bring into his fellowship those who come to him in faith, baptizing them in the Name of the Father, and of the Son, and of the Holy Spirit.

At the following words, the Celebrant touches the water.

Now sanctify this water, we pray you, by the power of your Holy Spirit, that those who here are cleansed from sin and born again may continue for ever in the risen life of Jesus Christ our Savior.

To him, to you, and to the Holy Spirit, be all honor and glory, now and for ever. *Amen.*

Commentary

A sermon could be preached on the theological depth of the Prayer of Thanksgiving over the water, which may be read with the blessing of the water at the beginning of the service or at the time appointed in the BCP.

As noted, music can also be key to enhancing the importance of the baptism service. Particular hymns and Eucharistic Prayers, as mentioned earlier, might be used exclusively for baptisms and used as reinforcement at other services that make a connection to the theme of baptism. There are a number of appropriate hymns appointed for All Saints' Day, Easter, Pentecost, and the Baptism of Our Lord. I personally recommend Hymn # 293, *I Sing a Song of the Saints of God*. Its message is appropriate, and children enjoy it. Considering all the visitors in attendance at a baptism, we might want to sing hymns that are familiar at least to the home congregation, if not to the visitors themselves. That is good hospitality. If the music at a baptism service is uplifting, then that excitement can influence the tone of voice of the leaders and the peoples' response. However, we also may not want to play a hymn with too many verses! Episcopalians are known for playing *all* verses.

Opening Acclamation

(adapted from BCP, 299)

Celebrant   There is one Body and one Spirit.
People   **There is one hope in God's call to us.**

Celebrant	One Lord, one Faith, one Baptism.
People	**One God and Father of all.**

Commentary

An acolyte carrying the Paschal candle leads the procession or comes immediately after the thurifer or verger. Another acolyte lights all the candles in the sanctuary from the Paschal candle and then it is placed in its stand near the altar. The baptismal bowl is placed on a table in front of the altar where the baptism will take place unless they intend to do the baptism at the back of the sanctuary. Another option is to stop three times and sing part of the Exsultet as an echo of the Easter Vigil.

The celebrant continues from the president's chair, or from where they would normally begin a service, with the opening acclamation. People are encouraged to respond with a strong voice.

The opening baptismal acclamation is taken from Paul's writings. "There is one faith, one baptism . . ." It is powerful and expresses the unity in baptism. It is hoped that these words will find their way into the hearts and souls of church members if said often enough. The celebrant may choose to say these words with that kind of passion, so that the responsorial acclamations between celebrant and people build to a crescendo. On these occasions and on Easter I repeat three times, "Alleluia, Christ is Risen!" and the people respond three times. They are now responding with great energy. On days when the baptismal vows are renewed, even without a baptism, it might be appropriate to begin the service with this opening acclamation, either by itself or in addition to the seasonal acclamation.

To highlight the opening acclamation, a preacher could consider sermonizing on the themes of one hope, one faith, one baptism. We find our oneness with Christ in participating in baptism and Eucharist, not in our doctrines and beliefs. Christ makes us one. We don't.

The Collects and Readings

(adapted from BCP collects, 254)

The celebrant reads the following Collect or the Collect of the Day or both, first saying

Celebrant   The Lord be with you.
People   **And also with you.**
Celebrant   Let us pray.

Almighty God, by our baptism into the death and resurrection of your Son Jesus Christ, you turn us from the old life of sin. Grant that we, being reborn to new life in him, may live in righteousness and holiness all our days; through Jesus Christ our Lord, who lives and reigns with you and the Holy Spirit, one God, now and forever. **Amen.**[10]

People sit.

The Lessons

The Gospel plus one or two lessons will be read. The Readings are selected from the suggested readings from a baptism listed in the lectionary for various occasions on page 928 of the BCP. The readings from the Proper of the Day may be used, especially if that Sunday is a significant feast day such as Pentecost, Feast of Transfiguration, Baptism of our Lord, Easter, etc.

Old Testament   Ezekiel 36:24–28 *or any of the other Old Testament Lessons from the Easter Vigil.*
Epistle   Romans 6:3–5 *or* Romans 8:14–17 *or* 2 Corinthians 5:17–20
Gospel   Mark 1:9–11 *or* Mark 10:13–16 *or* John 3:1–6

Commentary

Preaching on the same readings for every baptism is another way to reinforce the themes of baptism itself. After all, we use special appointed readings for funerals, weddings and ordinations. Repetition is a powerful tool. If you are concerned about the length of your service, consider having only two readings to save time, especially when adding other parts to a baptism service.

Response and Sermon

(adapted from BCP, 300–301)

The lector ends each lesson with,

---

10. BCP, 254.

"Hear what the Spirit is saying to God's people."

The people respond.

Thanks be to God.

After each lesson there may be silence. Lessons may be read by adults to be baptized as an actual way for them to move toward ministry in the church, much as is done by teenagers completing a bar mitzvah.

A psalm or hymn may be said or sung between readings.

All stand for the Gospel procession which is led with the Paschal candle, (and verger and thurifer if there is one), and a deacon or priest reads the Gospel, first saying:

The Holy Gospel of our Lord Jesus Christ according to . . . !

People   **Glory to you Lord Christ.**

After the Gospel, the reader says,

Hear what the Spirit is saying to God's people!

People   **Praise to you Lord Christ.**

Sermon *The sermon may be preached here or after the Peace.*

Commentary

The rite preaches! In his book *Planning the Church Year,* Leonel Mitchell reminds us, "Not only do the rites of Christian initiation deserve the best presentation we can give them . . . but they are an unparalleled opportunity for what the Church calls evangelism and what Madison Avenue calls advertising. People who come to the baptism of a friend or friend's child do not usually come prepared to be critical of either the service or the congregation."[11]

Using the "The Word of the Lord" at the end of each reading may hold different meanings for different members of the congregation. Visitors to the baptismal service who are unfamiliar with the service might draw the wrong conclusions about our view of scripture, especially in light of the

---

11. Leonel Mitchell, *Planning the Church Year* (Harrisburg, PA: Morehouse Publishing, 1991), 37.

popularity of fundamentalism and literalism. A better response might be to substitute what is being said in many congregations around the country: "Hear what the Spirit is saying to God's people!" These words come from an ancient document, *Didache*, dating from the first or second century.

The Exhortation

(adapted from the 1989 edition of *A New Zealand Prayer Book*, 384, part of the catechism at the back of the prayer book, scripture and some of my own insertions)

Celebrant

> The sacraments of Baptism and Eucharist were instituted by our Lord, and those who are called by His name have been baptizing those who came in faith since Peter gave his first sermon on the Day of Pentecost when three thousand people were immediately baptized. Peter said, "Repent and be baptized every one of you in the name of Jesus the Christ, for the forgiveness of sins and you will receive the Holy Spirit, for the promise is to you and to your children, to all who are far away, everyone who the Lord our God will call."[12]
>
> When the Holy Spirit fell upon Cornelius and his entire household, St. Peter said to his fellow Christians, "What is to prevent us from baptizing these persons?" We have been baptizing entire households since that time and baptizing infants and children reminds us that God loves us and calls us before we know what kind of person we will be and regardless of what kind of person we have become.
>
> The Ethiopian eunuch said to Philip, once Philip had interpreted the Scripture for him, "Here is some water! What is to prevent me from being baptized?" Philip immediately baptized him even though this person would not have been fully accepted into Judaism. This story reminds all of us who have been baptized that all are welcome and we are called

---

12. *A New Zealand Prayer Book* (Auckland: Collins, 1989), 384.

to proclaim by word and deed the Good News of God in Christ to all people and respect the dignity of every human being.

St. Paul said, "As many of you were baptized into Christ have clothed yourselves with Christ. There is no longer Jew and Greek, there is no longer slave or free, there is no longer male or female; for all of you are one in Christ Jesus. We are here reminded that having Christ in common overshadows all that would separate us from one another.

According to the words of St. John, "God so loved the world that he gave His only Son so that everyone who believes in him shall not perish but have everlasting life." St. John also writes, "We must be born of water and the Spirit to inherit the Kingdom of God."

The sacrament of Baptism is therefore not to be entered into lightly, for it is not only new birth for the baptized, but a call to ministry ... a ministry to represent Christ and His Church; to bear witness to Him wherever *they* may be; and according to the gifts given *them*, to carry on Christ's work of reconciliation in the world and to take *their* place in the life, worship and governance of the Church.

It will be *their* duty to join all of us in following Christ; coming together week by week for corporate worship; and working, praying and giving for the spread of the Kingdom of God.

Commentary

The celebrant invites the baptismal party forward and may suggest that the people remain seated so they can see. People often instinctively stand at this part of the service, though the prayer book gives no rubrics to do so. This is why the celebrant may invite the people to remain seated until the procession to the font, if there is a procession.

The celebrant, assistants, and acolyte with the Paschal candle gather in front. The celebrant says some or all of the following as the baptismal party is coming forward and says far less if the words from "the Call" (mentioned previously) was used. If the font is in front where people can remain seated and see, then it is recommended that the people remain seated until the welcoming of the newly baptized on page 308 of the BCP. This Call itself can replace the sermon or be the topic of several sermons.

Several parts of scripture are offered as instruction regarding baptism with the hope that these words may take hold in people.[13] These scriptures communicate some classic stories in scripture around baptism, beginning with Peter's first sermon about repenting and believing in Jesus Christ. The words from the Gospel of John connect baptism, rebirth, salvation, and the receiving of the Holy Spirit.

The fact that an Ethiopian eunuch was accepted for baptism makes a significant statement about inclusiveness in light of the exclusivity of Judaism. Some believe that the words of Paul from Galatians were part of the ancient baptismal ceremonies. This quote from Paul's letter to the Galatians 3:27–29 is one of the most inclusive and liberating comments that Paul makes, and these words remind us that the baptized are equal members of the Body of Christ and have equal access to all the rights, "rites," and privileges in the church. The story of Peter and Philip supports the immediacy of baptism without forcing the parents or the catechumen into a lengthy training program. *The "training program" comes with the lifelong journey of worshipping.*

The final two paragraphs come directly from the catechism on pages 855 and 856 of the Book of Common Prayer. The first is the answer to the question, "What is the ministry of the laity?" The second answers the question, "What is the duty of all Christians?" This is taking an opportunity for instruction for the whole parish. The laity may have read the catechism once during a confirmation or inquirers' class, but they probably haven't encountered it since. Hearing these duties repeated at every baptism and maybe even each time the baptismal vows are renewed might be effective stewardship of ministry and money.

Finally, readers should note the similarity in structure and tone to the "Comfortable Words" in Rite I on page 332 of the BCP. These were

---

13. Quoting scripture directly is also done in the sentences following the Absolution and preceding the Peace in Rite I on page 332 of the BCP.

repeated at every worship service when I was growing up and they comfort me today. Others may feel the same.

Presentation and Examination of Candidates

(adapted from BCP, 301)

The baptismal party turns and faces both the congregation and the celebrant.

Celebrant   The candidate(s) for Holy Baptism will now be presented.

Adults and Older Children

The candidates who are old enough to speak for themselves are presented individually by their sponsors. Sponsors speak loudly enough for the entire congregation to hear.

I present *N.* to receive the Sacrament of Baptism.

The celebrant asks each candidate when presented and the candidate responds so that the entire congregation can hear.

Celebrant   Do you desire to be baptized?
Catechumens   **I do.**

Infants and Younger Children

Each set of sponsors and/or Parents and Godparents present each individual saying in a strong voice:

I present *N.* to receive the Sacrament of Baptism.

Commentary

The celebrant stands between the baptismal party and the congregation, facing the candidates and with their back to the congregation so the celebrant is facing the baptismal party with the congregation because they are being presented to the congregation and priest. Usually the candidates turn their back on the congregation and face the celebrant, who is facing them and the congregation. They might gather in front of the altar or the steps to the altar. This will also help the congregation see and hear all those involved. It is not clear from our Book of Common Prayer if in fact the candidates are being presented to the congregation or to the celebrant, who may represent the congregation. It is spelled out in *Common Worship* on page 352 that they are presented to the congregation and not to the celebrant, so once all the candidates have come forward, they face the congregation and the celebrant. The Presentation and Examination of Candidates is concluded with the last collect from the Easter Vigil service (BCP, 291).[14]

I recommend printing headings in bold type for the presentation of other candidates and congregational response. This creates "liturgical space on paper" and quite frankly, it's a good reminder to the celebrant if there are other candidates. We who are in charge sometimes forget.

Renunciations and Proclamations

(adapted from BCP, 302–303)

When all have been presented, the Celebrant then addresses the parents and/or Godparents. Answers are given in strong, bold, definite tones.

Celebrant   Will you be responsible for seeing that the child you present is brought up in the Christian life and faith?
Answer   **I will with God's help!**

Celebrant   Will you by your prayers and witness help this child to grow into the full stature of Christ?
Answer   **I will with God's help!**

The celebrant may choose at any time to simply say, "Repeat after me!" breaking up each sentence so that the candidates are able to recite the words of the vows and commitments.

Renunciations

Question   Do you renounce Satan and all the spiritual forces of wickedness that rebel against God?
Answer   **I renounce them!**

14. It is also said at ordination services (BCP, 515, 528, 540) following the presentation and litany and it is the last solemn collect said on Good Friday (BCP, 280). A similar prayer is said by the minister after the final baptismal vow is made in The Church of England's alternative prayer book, *Common Worship*.

Question	Do you renounce all the evil powers of this world which corrupt and destroy the creatures of God?
Answer	**I renounce them!**
Question	Do you renounce all sinful desires that draw you from the love of God?
Answer	**I renounce them!**

Proclamations[15]

Question	Do you turn to Jesus Christ and accept Him as your savior?
Answer	**I do!**
Question	Do you put your whole trust in His grace and love?
Answer	**I do!**
Question	Do you promise to follow and obey Him as your Lord?
Answer	**I do!**

Commentary

An alternative way of reciting the proclamations is for the celebrant to say, "Repeat after me!"

"I accept Jesus Christ as my Lord and Savior!"

"I put my whole trust in his Grace and love!"

"I promise to follow and obey him as my Lord!"

The celebrant can break up the renunciations into shorter segments as is done in a wedding. Having the candidates or their godparents actually recite the proclamations, rather than saying, "I do!" or "I will!" makes it more personal.

A sermon on any of these renunciations, proclamations, or the final prayer could be given. Ask yourself and your congregation: What are you renouncing in this society? What is being raised up? What does it mean to trust and turn to Jesus Christ?

---

15. Marion Hatchett calls this "The Act of Adherence." In the Eastern catechetical instructions of Cyril of Jerusalem and John Chrysostom of Antioch, the threefold renunciation of Satan was followed by a threefold act of adherence to Christ. In some rites of renunciation of Satan, the candidate was facing west as a sign of rejection. The candidate then turned to the East, which signified light and life and the eschaton, for the act of adherence. (Hatchett, *Commentary*, 270–271.).

Presentation of Other Candidates

(adapted from BCP, 303)

When there are others to be presented, the celebrant speaks so the entire congregation can hear.

Celebrant	The other candidate(s) will now be presented.
Presenters	I present *these persons* for Confirmation. I present *these persons* to be received into this communion. I present *these persons* who desire to reaffirm *their* baptismal vows.

The Celebrant asks the candidate(s):

Question	Do you reaffirm your renunciation of evil?
Answer	**I do!**
Question	Do you renew your commitment to Jesus Christ?
Answer	**I do, and with God's Grace, I will follow Him as my Savior and Lord!**

Congregational Response

After all have been presented, the Celebrant addresses the congregation, saying:

Question	Will you who witness these vows do all in your power to support *these persons* in *their* life in Christ?
Answer	**We will!**
Celebrant	Let us pray!

O God of unchangeable power and eternal light: Look favorably on your whole Church, that wonderful and sacred mystery; by the effectual working of your providence, carry out in tranquility the plan of salvation; let the whole world see and know that things which were cast down are being raised up, and things which have grown old are being made new, and that all things are being brought to their perfection by Him through whom all things were made, Your Son Jesus Christ our Lord; who lives and reigns with you in the unity of the Holy Spirit, one God, for ever and ever. **Amen!**

Commentary

The last prayer above is taken from the ordination service, and serves as another reminder to examine the services for ordination in order to incorporate aspects into a baptism service, as much more pageantry has been put into ordination services than the baptism service.

Inserting the voice rubrics for the participants may be helpful reminders for them to speak up, since they may be nervous and forget what they were told during the rehearsal. Including a large print bulletin with clear instructions for the baptismal party might be helpful.

Regarding the vow of all who witness this, I remind the congregation ahead of time that this includes giving to the church to sustain programs for all as they grow in the Lord. I then add (with humor) the duties of babysitting and driving kids to soccer in order to help the parents. Occasionally paying for their college education might be an obligation. Their response is all caps to emphasize their enthusiastic response.

The Baptismal Covenant

(adapted from BCP, 304–305)

The Celebrant then says these words or similar words.

Please stand and let us join with *those* who are committing *themselves* to Christ and renew our own baptismal covenant by professing what we believe and then what we will do because of what we believe.

Profession of Faith[16]

Celebrant	Do you believe in God the Father?
People	**I believe in God the Father . . .**
Celebrant	Do you believe in Jesus Christ, the Son of God?
People	**I believe in Jesus Christ . . .**
Celebrant	Do you believe in God the Holy Spirit?
People	**I believe in the Holy Spirit . . .**

---

16. Entire recitation is found on page 304 of the Book of Common Prayer.

The Baptismal Vows: A Model for Discipleship

Celebrant

Repeat after me.

Celebrant breaks up the sentence and leads the congregation in reciting one brief part of the vows after another, so the congregation can repeat it.

We will with God's help, continue in the apostles' teaching and fellowship, in the breaking of bread, and in the prayers!

We will with God's help, persevere in resisting evil, and whenever we fall into sin, repent and return to the Lord!

We will with God's help, proclaim by word and example, the Good News of God in Christ!

We will with God's help, seek and serve Christ in all people, loving our neighbor as ourselves!

We will with God's help, strive for justice and peace, respecting the dignity of every human being!

Celebrant   May the Lord who has given you the will to do these things, give you the grace and power to perform them!

People   **Amen!**

Commentary

The inspiration for sermons can be found in all of this part of the service! For example, one could preach on "What we believe and what we will do because of our belief."

Asking the congregation to repeat the entire vow, rather than a simple "We will!" will help them learn the vows. We already do this at weddings. Not only does this resolve the problem of candidates having to look down at a book as they make these important promises to God and the congregation, but separating them into short repetitive phrases gives proper emphasis to each phrase or clause.

The concluding prayer is taken from the ordination services. It is said by the bishop at ordinations after the candidates have made their vows

(BCP, 532). It is an especially appropriate prayer to be said after making our baptismal vows.

Prayers and Procession to the Font

(adapted from BCP, 305–306)

Celebrant

Let us pray for *these persons* who are to receive the Sacrament of new birth and for those who will be companions with them on their journey of faith.

A person appointed leads the petitions (pages 305–306). The bracketed prayer is said if there are Parents or Godparents.

Celebrant

[Faithful and loving God, bless those who care for these children and grant them your gifts of love, wisdom and faith. Pour upon them your healing and reconciling love and protect their home from evil. Fill them with the light of your presence and establish them in the joy of your Kingdom, through Jesus Christ our Lord.] **AMEN!**

Procession to the Font

Celebrant

All are invited to join in the procession to the baptismal font. Those who might have a difficult time viewing the baptism, such as small children, are particularly encouraged to join the procession first so that they might see better.

Commentary

It is appropriate that one or more of the sponsors reads the prayers for the candidates. The procession to the font may take place during this litany in which case the invitation offered below is read before the prayers. The font may be in front or at the back of the nave so processions may be short or lengthy. The acolyte carries the Paschal candle, possibly led by the thurifer or verger.[17]

---

17. A thurifer carries the incense and a verger is master of ceremonies who usually leads processions.

It has been suggested by Louis Weil in a booklet by Associated Parishes that the procession to the font may begin during the prayers.[18] The idea for adding the prayer for parents and godparents came from an online liturgical chat group I participate in. It can help in a little way to reinforce their special call, and they can use the extra prayers. I obtained this prayer from *Common Worship*, page 358.

For the procession, everyone stands. If the font is in front, then the people may remain seated so they can see. At the point of actual baptism, it will be important for the celebrant to invite the small children who want to get a closer look. The acolyte takes the Paschal candle and follows immediately behind the thurifer and verger (if there is one) leading the baptismal party to the font. Psalm 42 or some other appropriate psalm or hymn may be said or sung in place of the Prayers over the Candidates as the procession moves toward the font.

Pitchers or vases full of water that are visible to the congregation and large enough to fill the font to the brim are poured into the font by either acolytes or members of the baptismal party as the celebrant reads or sings the thanksgiving prayer, if it had not already been blessed at the beginning of the service. If the font is too small to receive all that water, then the celebrant may bless the water in all the pitchers so parishioners can take some home with them after the service.

The Baptism

(adapted from BCP, 307–308)

A hymn praying for the Holy Spirit, such as "Veni Sancte Spiritus," may be sung at this point as the people wait in silence.

The celebrant usually stands facing the congregation across the font. Each candidate is presented by name to the Celebrant, or to an assisting priest or deacon, who then immerses, or pours water upon the candidate, saying:

N., I baptize you in the name of the Father

The candidate is immersed or has water poured upon them a second time.

---

18. *Holy Baptism: A Liturgical and Pastoral Commentary* (Alexandria, VA: Associated Parishes, 1991).

And the Son,

The candidate is immersed or has water poured upon them a final time.

And the Holy Spirit!

When these actions have been completed for all the candidates, the Bishop or Priest, at a place in full sight of the congregation, prays over them, saying

Let us pray:

Heavenly Father, we thank you that by water and the Holy Spirit you have bestowed upon *these* your *servants* the forgiveness of sin and have raised *them* to the new life of grace. Sustain *them*, O Lord, in your Holy Spirit. Give *them* an inquiring and discerning heart, the courage to will and to persevere, a spirit to know and to love you, and the gift of joy and wonder in all your works.

Amen.

Commentary

The rubrics from page 552 of the BCP recommend the hymns to the Holy Spirit for ordinations just before the actual ordination takes place. *Veni Creator Spiritus* or *Veni Sancte Spiritus* are recommended. Baptism is supposed to be when we first receive the Holy Spirit, so these hymns are quite appropriate and powerful. They emphasize the moment providing a solemn pause in the liturgy. The font should be censed during this hymn. A period of silent prayer follows, the people still standing as able.

We have now reached the pinnacle of the service so far. *Baptisms are why we are here* and that is why in the rubric above I recommend that the fonts are larger, and the baptism is divided into three parts. We want the actual act of baptizing to stand out in the bulletin and in the service!

The celebrant may allow her voice to reflect that this is the climax of what are doing. Adult catechumens were immersed three times in many early churches. In some cities they would profess their faith by saying some part of what we know as the Apostles' Creed before each immersion.[19]

---

19. Hatchett, *Commentary on the Book of Common Prayer*, 253–254.

I believe in God the Father ... first immersion.

I believe in Jesus Christ, the Son of God ... second immersion.

I believe in God, the Holy Spirit ... final immersion.

Separating these immersions (pourings) in the bulletin with rubrics and space helps highlight the baptism itself. We should take our time and let the words reflect that. The current layout of the service in the BCP gives only one line to the actual baptism and it almost disappears within the rest of the print. Image matters on so many levels.

So how much water? Do we splash, pour, sprinkle or immerse? I suggest, "The more the merrier!" The BCP puts immersion first in the rubrics, which means that it is the expected norm. Immersions can include pouring a lot of water over the person. Submersion is putting the candidate completely under water. Each congregation will do what is congruent with its life and culture. However, it must be remembered that baptism is not to be compared to a "dainty act of putting one's toe in water," but more like "running and leaping" into the water. I have held adults and older children's faces in the bowl (for only one second) to give the image of "going down into the water" and as they gasp between the three immersions, it makes an impression on the people.

The Anointing with Oil and the Laying on of Hands
(adapted from BCP, 307)

The acolyte, carrying the Paschal candle, then leads the baptismal party to the altar.[20] Psalm 23 or some other appropriate psalm or hymn may be sung as the procession moves. If the celebrant plans to sprinkle the congregation with the blessed water, helpers carry several basins of the blessed water in the procession.

An acolyte, who is holding the oil of chrism, removes the stopper and hands the oil to the celebrant.[21] The bishop has previously blessed the oil, so the celebrant omits the bracketed part of the prayer. This may all be done immediately after the administration of water and before the preceding prayer. It would be appropriate for the celebrant to give a bit of instruction on chrism at this point.

---

20. This was recommended in trial services from 1973 (*Authorized Services*, 33).

21. The oil of chrism may be placed upon the altar ahead of time in which case the acolyte retrieves it.

Celebrant

Eternal Father, whose blessed Son was anointed by the Holy Spirit to be the Savior and servant of all, we pray ["You to consecrate this oil"], that those who are sealed with this oil of chrism, may share in the royal priesthood of Jesus Christ; who lives and reigns with you and the Holy Spirit, for ever and ever. **AMEN!**

The Laying on of Hands

The celebrant may invite the whole baptismal party to lay hands upon the newly baptized.

N., *I/we* lay *my/our* hands upon you in the name of the Father, and of the Son and of the Holy Spirit.

The Anointing with Oil

The use of chrism/blessed oil which is optional, signifies the cleansing of sins, the biblical anointing of kings and priests, and the "seal" of the Holy Spirit in baptism and incorporation into Christ, which title means, "The Anointed One." The word "christens" derived from the chrism: to be "christened" is to be "anointed." Because the oil of chrism can be consecrated only by the bishop, its use in the absence of the bishop signifies the relationship of the bishop's office of baptism.[22]

Some congregations may leave the large cruet of oil on display most every Sunday, whether at the font or on the altar or some other appropriate place.

The celebrant either makes the sign of the cross on the forehead of the newly baptized using the chrism of oil or pours oil over their heads, while the baptismal party keeps their hands on the baptized. The celebrant says:

"You are sealed by the Holy Spirit in Baptism and marked as Christ's own forever!"

People   **AMEN!**

---

22. Hatchett, 281.

Commentary

We could preach a sermon on receiving the Holy Spirit or on the eternal mark of baptism. Clarifying Paul's statement that nothing can separate us from the love of God would also be appropriate.

We do not always think to look closely at the rubrics as we prepare for the next stage in a long service like this. The anointing with oil and laying on of hands can get lost in the current rubrics of the BCP. The rite of anointing with oil and laying on of hands are two of the most ancient traditions and deserve their own heading.[23] *The New Zealand Prayer Book* actually includes a heading for the Laying on of Hands in the table of contents as well as within the context of the liturgy itself, which helps clue the parishioners in on what is happening.[24] Often, most parishioners cannot see the laying on of hands, nor the small vial of oil or the actual anointing.[25]

The rubrics allow for the anointing of the newly baptized immediately after baptizing them with water, so it is not too inconvenient to wait until after the first prayer. The prayer of consecration of the oil reminds all of us that we participate in the royal priesthood of Jesus Christ, so it is good to pray even when the bishop is not present, or if the bishop is present and is using previously consecrated oil. The bracketed part of the prayer above can be omitted if the oil has already been blessed.

There is no rubric preventing the entire baptismal party from joining the celebrant in laying on of hands, and this image can be powerful. When an infant is baptized it can be appropriate that the baby be passed from one person to another. Official representatives could be a part of this, with their names printed in the bulletin. What a wonderful outward and visible symbol of baptismal ministry.

The Asperges

If not done earlier in the service, the celebrant or representatives of ministries within the congregations may then take one or two leafy evergreen branches

---

23. Hatchett, *Commentary*, 278–281.
24. *A New Zealand Prayer Book* (Auckland: Collins), 1989.
25. Creating a visible space and place somewhere near the altar for a large chrism of oil will at least get people to ask "What is it?" from time to time.

or an aspergillum[26] *and while a helper carries a bowl of the blessed baptismal water, sprinkles the baptismal water over the baptismal party and congregation as they lead the baptismal party back toward the altar, repeating over and over again as they splash water saying:*

Remember that you have been sealed by the Holy Spirit in Baptism and marked as Christ's own forever!

Commentary

The asperges is optional, but I can tell you from experience that the people highly value this part of the service of Holy Baptism, which I have been doing for years. It would be a good thing to have several basins of water and several people to sprinkle water so that this is done in an efficient manner. The sprinkling can take place during the procession to the altar, or it can take place afterwards as is suggested in this service.

When I do this the people often bow in anticipation of the water being splashed upon them, and they are learning the words, and often recite them as I say the words, "Sealed by the Holy Spirit in Baptism and marked as Christ's own forever!" I would say this has been one of the more transforming parts of the service. We sing a beautiful "Spirit" song as it is done, and it is the same song we sing as we pause just before the actual baptism. I use both hands and splash both sides of the aisle.

Welcome

When all have been baptized and anointed with oil and received the laying on of hands, the celebrant says:

Let us welcome the newly baptized!

The people, if seated, should now stand.

Celebrant and People

We receive you into the household of God. Confess the faith of Christ crucified, proclaim his resurrection and share with us in his eternal priesthood!

---

26. An aspergillum is a metal cylinder that is dipped into the water and holds enough water to splash the people.

Applause is appropriate at this time and celebrative instrumental music may be played immediately after this and/or during the asperges if they occur. If there is to be Confirmation, Reception, or the Reaffirmation of Baptismal Vows, the rites and prayers from pages 309–310 of the BCP immediately follow the applause.

Commentary

"You are marked as Christ's own forever and don't you forget it!" Personally, I recommend saying this to the ones baptized and to the entire congregation at every baptism or renewal of vows when water is splashed on the congregation.

   I have noticed that usually, unless steps are taken, this point in many baptismal services is anticlimactic rather than climatic. Adding vibrant music, applause, and the asperges adds to the climax of this aspect of the service. One of the primary aspects of baptism is the incorporation of the baptized into the Body of Christ, so this welcome could appropriately be a rousing liturgical moment.

Presentation of Gifts

Various gifts, including the signed baptismal, confirmation, reaffirmation and/or reception certificate(s) are presented by the sponsors or representatives of the congregation. Some gifts might be given later at a reception in the parish hall. This part will be omitted if there are no gifts.

Celebrant   Let us pray.

Everliving God, whose power is limitless, we place before you, with our praise and thanks, *these tokens* of your *servant's* ministry and dignity . . .

Gifts may be presented

The Baptismal Certificate . . . Remember your baptism!
A candle . . . Be the light of the world! (*Candle is lit from the Paschal candle.*)
A banner . . . You are sealed by the Holy Spirit in Baptism and marked as Christ's own forever!
A Prayer Book . . . Pray unceasingly!
A towel . . . Serve the world!
A quilt or blanket or shawl . . . You are surrounded by love and prayers!

Grant that *N (s)* who *has* been called to join in the priesthood of all believers in your Church and bears these signs, may faithfully serve you and share in the fullness of your life-giving Spirit; through the High Priest and Good Shepherd of us all, Jesus Christ our Lord. **AMEN**.

Commentary

This rubric echoes ordination services, and the marks of authority a newly ordained person or a newly installed rector receives. Our congregation gives beautiful blankets or framed gifts to the newly baptized. They include the name and date and the words "You have been sealed by the Holy spirit in Baptism and marked as Christ's own forever!"

The Peace, Prayers of the People, Offertory, and the Eucharist

(adapted from BCP, 308–310)

Celebrant	The peace of the Lord be always with you.
People	**And also with you.**

The entire congregation may choose to come forward to exchange the peace with the newly baptized. Once the baptismal party has exchanged the peace with one another, they take their seats.

The "Prayers of the People" may be omitted or read at this point. The newly baptized or their representatives may read them as a sign of their taking part in ministry immediately, as they pray for the Church and the world. The celebrant may conclude the prayers with the Collect for baptism on page 395 of the BCP. Eucharistic Prayer D on pages 372–376, includes prayers for the world, so if the Prayers of the People are omitted, this Eucharistic Prayer would be appropriate.

The service continues with the Offertory and Eucharist, at which the Bishop, when present, should be the principal celebrant. Some congregations may choose to use one particular Eucharistic Prayer for Baptisms and the Proper Preface for baptisms may be used.[27] *Special seasonal post Communion Prayers may be*

---

27. *Common Worship,* 362.

used.[28] *The celebrant may invite the baptismal party to gather around the Lord's Table for the Great Thanksgiving, in which case the baptismal party will receive Communion first and then return to their seats.*

Commentary

If the newly baptized are old enough, they could be encouraged to go out into the congregation to exchange the Peace. The newly baptized with their family could bring forward the oblations.[29]

The Prayers of the People may be read at this point or may be omitted since the prayers for the candidates have been read and if one wants to shorten the length of the service. However, the Prayers for the Candidates do not include prayers for the church and the world. Part of their preparation could have been in the writing of these prayers.

Having the baptismal party immediately come up around the altar makes clear that baptism is complete initiation into the life of the church. It could be a model for inviting others up around the altar on a regular basis, such as when new ministries are commissioned. This is recommended in the book *The Catechumenate*, which is a commentary on the Catechumenate[30] in *The Book of Occasional Services.*[31]

One may choose a special Eucharistic Prayer to always use at baptisms as a way through repetition to remind them of the specialness and uniqueness of baptisms. I happen to use Prayer C, because it is beautiful and might appeal to visitors and congregants alike, as it is usually not the primary prayer churches use.

Procession, Dismissal, Reception, and Fellowship

The crucifer leads the procession out with the cross while a hymn is sung by the congregation. The celebrant may invite the baptismal party to join in the procession. The deacon or celebrant, standing next to the font, makes the dismissal.

---

28. *Common Worship*, 362.
29. These are the gifts of bread, wine and financial offerings.
30. This is an intense program of education and formation that might be used for those wanting to be baptized.
31. *The Catechumenate: Formation for Church Membership,* (Alexandria, VA: Associated Parishes, 1991), 11.

The Song of Simeon

This may be sung by a soloist or chanted by the congregation.

Lord, you now have set your servant free
to go in peace as you have promised;

For these eyes of mine have seen the Savior,
whom you have prepared for all the world to see:

A Light to enlighten the nations,
And the glory of your people Israel.

All say together

Glory to the Father and to the Son and to the Holy Spirit, as it was in the beginning is now and will be forever!

Deacon or Celebrant

Let us go forth into the world rejoicing in the power of the Spirit! Alleluia! Alleluia!

People   **THANKS BE TO GOD! ALLELUIA! ALLELUIA!**

The congregation may be invited to follow the procession directly to the fellowship hall for announcements and a reception. Bottles may be available for dipping into the font in order to take some blessed water home.[32]

Commentary

The Song of Simeon communicates a sense of fulfillment for all that this day has been. Recited when Jesus was brought to the temple as an infant, it recalls both a culmination of hopes and dreams and the potential in the baby Jesus and for the one baptized. Across the country, the people are adding two alleluias, and I don't doubt they will appear in future authorized versions.

---

32. My wife's family took home water from the baptismal font in their Roman Catholic parish in Pittsburgh when she was growing up.

Believer's Baptism: Reaffirming of Vows

(adapted from BCP, 303, regarding "reaffirming their vows" . . .)

Arrangements may be made for those who were baptized as infants and want to experience what is popularly called, a "believer's baptism." We believe "once baptized, always baptized" and that we are baptized into the "one holy catholic and apostolic church" and not into one denomination. We do not officially do second baptisms. This "believer's baptism" option is a renewal of the Baptismal Covenant and vows but pastorally offers the opportunity to experience something outward and visible that one who is already baptized can remember. These candidates will have also said the renunciations and proclamations and recited the Baptismal Covenant and vows with the other candidates and congregation.

Celebrant   [*Name*], Remember!

Candidate dunks face into the water the first time.

Celebrant   You have been sealed by the Holy Spirit in Baptism

Candidate dunks face in the water a second time.

Celebrant   And marked as Christ's own forever!

Candidate dunks face in water a third time.

Celebrant   And don't you ever forget it!

Commentary

These rubrics are included in the service almost as an invitation to adults in the congregation to consider this option. I have heard adults say they almost resent being baptized as infants because they missed out on remembering the experience.

Developing Your Own Template

Taking the time needed to enhance a service of Holy Baptism might be a great challenge for clergy and staff of congregations who currently are too busy with other duties to invest the amount of time and energy to plan liturgies like this. It can be done though, for I have been doing it for years.

Once you have the format you can simply use it for every baptism. Every time I review this book, I am reminded to implement more ideas from it.

Questions for Reflection

1. What do you think of processing the Paschal candle in at the beginning of the service and Gospel procession, while processing the cross at the end of the service?

2. Have you noticed the laying on of hands or anointing with oil at baptisms or have those actions been invisible?

3. What gifts does your congregation give, or what new gifts can you imagine giving?

4. Remembering that this is "over the top," what parts of the above could be effective in your congregation?

5. Did any of the suggestions surprise, shock, or inspire you? Why?

CHAPTER 7

Architecture and Accoutrements

The Font

The placement and/or enhancement of the font and its multiple uses speaks volumes about how a congregation lives into baptism. Where we stand and when we speak or act matters. What a font looks like matters.

Too often, I have had to search for the font in churches I have visited.

Too often, they are off in a corner waiting to be pulled out for a baptism.

Too often, books and cups of coffee are found placed upon them.

Too often, they have no water in them and are covered by an ornate lid.

Too often, they are too small for a bird to get a complete bath.

Blessing fresh water in the font from time to time brings attention to the font and to the blessing prayer. Altar guilds have asked me to bless extra water after the service, but I always do it during the service, so the people know what is going on.

Placing a large and beautiful bowl over the tiny opening on a font can enhance its prominence. Having an acolyte lift and carry the full bowl of water as the celebrant uses evergreen branches and splashes the congregation enhances the meaning and power of the service. One can even bring the bowl down to the front of the church and place it on a holder so the baptism can take place in front of the people. All of this can take place without the expense of building a full-size baptismal font in the floor of the church.

We at our church have a large bowl sitting upon the font located at the back of the nave: the bowl enhances the size but is also available for carrying throughout the church. We bless the water at the beginning of a baptism service and then carry the bowl in procession as we splash the waters on the people. Finally, we place the bowl on a table just in front of the altar so that when the baptism happens it happens in sight of everyone. Too often it is a hinderance for people to turn backwards in their pews to watch a baptism at the back of the church.

Professor Christopher Duraisingh from the Episcopal Divinity School suggests that the church should be seen primarily as an armory for training for mission. Though I agree with Dr. Duraisingh's ideals, I do not think the majority of church members see it that way. Too often the Israelites were more interested in seeing themselves as the chosen people of God rather than chosen to be "a light unto the nations," a holy priesthood for the nations. Likewise, we Christians often see ourselves as the redeemed, and forget that we are redeemed to be salt and light for the world.

I view the baptismal font as neither both/and nor either/or entrance and exit. The baptismal font is a much richer symbol than one that represents just one or two realities. Baptism represents both our need for cleansing and our commission for ministry, so beginning and ending all services at the font may be appropriate. It also represents our dying and rising with Christ, our receiving the Holy Spirit, being incorporated into the Body of Christ, and so much more. For these reasons, beginning the service at the font at funerals, weddings, ordinations, and other special services may be appropriate. Likewise, dismissals can be given from the font.

Our words of dismissal can be words of comfort, challenge, formation, or fortification in a particular season or on a particular occasion. Each dismissal and each opening prayer might emphasize a particular aspect of the symbolism of baptism. On any given Sunday it would be appropriate to communicate the values of mission and ministry as we pass the font on our way into the world. An educational placard for each season could be placed at the foot of the font so people would read it as they left church. There are many prayers, such as prefaces and collects (BCP, 157–261) and other denominational resources that can serve as entrance and exit prayers.

The font itself and its place and space make a strong statement for baptismal formation. Placing the Paschal candle next to the font as its regular place of prominence would help highlight both the font and the candle. *One would hope that anyone who attends a service will see and experience the importance of baptism simply by observing the location and prominence of the baptismal font.* Some pews may have to be removed in order to set aside holy space around the font. After all, most congregations do not cram a tiny altar into a tiny space. A small font is not where the *ultimate bath* should be held.[1]

An effort to create space where many can gather around the font to witness the baptism is encouraged. The majority of congregations are small, so there might be creative ways to provide a space where all can see, though this may not be practical in larger congregations. Chairs could replace a few pews that are closest to the font, which would then allow flexibility in the space when a baptism is scheduled.[2] This would reassure those who want extra seating for weddings and funerals.

Ideally the font is large enough to require a number of pitchers or jars or vases to fill it to the brim. The many pitchers of water bring to mind Jesus's first miracle at Cana, turning water in the large jars into wine. Surely the waters of baptism and the anointing of the Holy Spirit in baptism are all about new wine! Large jars full of the blessed waters of baptism could be placed on either side of the font so members could dip a container in and take it home. God's grace is overflowing and there is nothing held back. Overflowing and splashing on the floor should bring a bit of shock and surprise, followed by smiles.

Congregations must ask themselves, "What does our font say about the symbols and values of baptisms?" A portable font rolled into the corner of the narthex that is used as a bookshelf until an actual baptism unfortunately reinforces the concept that baptisms are a one-shot deal, and are only about the one being baptized.

Our church, like so many churches, has many entrances. The font is located at the original formal entrance into the nave. However, after the parking lot was installed twenty years ago, 95 percent of the members enter through the parish hall. The question arises, "Where is the real entrance?" Where should a font be located if the goal is to have it intentionally placed where everyone will pass by it? Should there be a font at

---

1. I have seen them used as a place to store books or leave bulletins. I do not think altars should be used this way.

2. The memorial plaques that were attached to the removed pews could be attached to other pews or a new plaque dedicating the holy space could include the names that were on the removed pews.

each entrance? Having only one font is a better symbol of "one faith, one hope, one baptism," but what good is it if we do not regularly educate the congregation about the symbolism of baptism being the entrance into the one holy catholic church? Congregations are encouraged to explore placing their font in other spaces if it will provide an opportunity for continuing education.

Preachers should remind the congregation of the stoups, which are small containers of baptismal water attached to the walls at the entrances/exits of the sanctuary. Typically, people dip their fingers in them and make the sign of the cross as they come and go. This can be an outward and visible reminder of their baptism and what it means. Encourage your congregation to try it!

Location, appearance, and the surroundings of the font should and will reflect either the conscious or unconscious meanings of baptism as perceived by those responsible for liturgical leadership. Placing the font at the front has been a popular liturgical move in the last forty or so years. In this position it is seen by all worshippers, along with the altar and the pulpit, and at least parishioners walk by the font as they come to the communion rail. Liturgical gurus will give great and confident reasons for locating the font in the narthex, up front with the pulpit and altar, or some other location. There is no absolute in that, but those in leadership need to give a solid liturgical reason for its location and appearance with ongoing education about it. The following are some suggestions for both:

- Locate the font at the entrance to the nave reflecting our entrance into the church and our exit to ministry.
- Locate the font in an elevated position at the front of the church so everyone can see a baptism and/or walk by it on their way to receive communion. This, like the BCP, connects baptism with Holy Communion and visibly links baptism to the altar, pulpit, and font.
- Create space for many people to gather around the font when the baptism takes place. It is so powerful when people stand shoulder to shoulder with acolytes, torches, candles, oil, and water to welcome the newest children of God.
- Place a large baptismal banner next to the font at all times, and use that banner for processions when there is to be a baptism.

The Asperges . . . Splashing the People!

The asperges—splashing of water—can help us remember our baptism, and I have found this to be one of the most effective ways to reach the people in the pew regarding the celebratory nature of baptism or simply renewing our baptismal vows. They can be performed from the font at services of reaffirmation or, as in some highly ritualistic parishes, every Sunday at the beginning of the service.[3] The celebrant may say some words from the baptismal service, such as:

Remember that through the waters of baptism you have been buried with Christ in his death, raised with Christ in his resurrection, and reborn by the Holy Spirit.

There is one Body, one Spirit, one Hope in God's call to us, one Lord, one Faith, one Baptism, one God and Father of all!

Remember you have been sealed by the Holy Spirit in Baptism and marked as Christ's own forever!

The first few times I did this, the congregants were surprised, and some smiled and even thought it funny. Now they bow as they are splashed, and they do remember the words said over them. It especially adds to the celebratory drama of an actual baptism.

Blessing Water

Our altar guild is always asking me to bless fresh water for the font (please keep the font full of water year-round except maybe Lent and Advent!) or the stoups at the entrances to the sanctuary, which hold holy water. Originally, I would bless a milk carton full of water in the sacristy. This is almost sacrilege! Taking our lead from the Easter Vigil, we now bless the fresh water either on the altar or at the font whenever needed, though I always try to connect liturgical actions to liturgical seasons.

Connecting Font to Hearth

Keeping blessed water in the font most seasons of the year can help remind people of their baptism year-round. What after all does an

---

3. My friend Fr. William Willoughby does this every Sunday.

empty baptismal font represent? Congregations could consider keeping the font full of water especially if new water is blessed every time congregations renew their baptismal vows. Having immersed myself in baptismal imagery, I always find it odd to enter a church where the font is dry.

In addition, inviting all households to dip bottles into the font and to take that water home can help make connections between church and home.[4] It also encourages parishioners to set aside vessels at home that they can fill from these bottles. These vessels could be set near their doors so that every day they come and go, they can dip their fingers in the water, make the sign of the cross, and recount some simple words from the liturgy, depending on the season,

In Epiphany: *I am Christ's own forever!*
In Advent: *May I do justice, love mercy and walk humbly with my God!*
In Lent: *Lord have Mercy!*
In Pentecost: *The joy of the Lord is my strength!*
In Easter: *Alleluia! Christ is risen!*
In the fall season after Pentecost: *Christ beside me, Christ before me, Christ above me, Christ below me!*

Educators could provide liturgies for home blessings with the water. The hearth at home can be connected and reconnected to the church font, altar, and ambo (a lectern used for all readings and preaching), in order to help build up a worshipping community of Christians.[5] The *Lambeth Report of 1948* reminds parents and godparents that they are responsible to raise their children to understand the faith. The primary job of teaching belongs to them.[6] Families can pour the water into sacred vessels that were made in Sunday school. Providing prayers to go with anything they do with water at home would help reinforce the values of baptism. Jewish people have many rituals around water to remind them of their relationship with God. The beauty of water is that, like bread, we need and

---

4. Read Klara Tammany's book *Living Water, Baptism as a Way of Life*, for ideas for the home. (See Bibliography.)
5. E.W. Southcott, *Receive this Child* (London: A.R. Mowbray & Co., 1951), 28.
6. Ibid.

encounter it every day, whether drinking, bathing, washing dishes, washing hands, or watering plants.

The Paschal Candle

The Paschal candle, which is lit at the Great Easter Vigil, is a symbol of the light of Christ in the world and yet represents so much more. There are numerous opportunities to use this powerful symbol of the Paschal Feast, such as the crucifixion and resurrection, but too often the Paschal candle goes unnoticed. Congregations that internalize the values of baptism may begin asking questions like, "Why not take a lead from the Easter Vigil and process in with the Paschal candle at every baptism service, or at every service during the Easter season or at every Sunday service other than Lent?" Why not echo the sounds from the Easter Vigil procession of the Paschal candle on page 285 of the BCP, pausing three times to say or sing, "The light of Christ!" with the people responding, "Thanks be to God!"

Associated Parishes published a number of booklets around 1980, several of which recommended that an acolyte or deacon process with the Paschal candle at baptisms.[7] The cross is a crucial symbol representing the crucifixion and resurrection, while our own death with Christ and our own resurrection are represented in baptism. Why not process in with the Paschal candle and process out with the cross? Processing in with the Paschal candle and then processing out with the cross can be a powerful statement of our entering church through the waters of baptism and leaving church in the way of the cross. The Rev. Donald Chapman elaborates upon the many meanings of the Paschal candle in his doctoral thesis, "The Eight Faces of Baptism":

> It bears witness to the Passover of Christ, the crucifixion and the resurrection. The Greek letters, Alpha and Omega, are imprinted upon it and they signify Christ as the beginning and the end of our lives and of the lives of everyone. The spikes in the candle represent the nails in our Lord at the crucifixion.

> At the Easter Vigil when the candle is lighted, the celebrant proclaims that the light of Christ drives out all darkness from the

---

7. See Associated Parishes in the bibliography.

hearts and minds of the worshippers. It recalls the pilgrimage of the Jews from the land of Egypt through the Red Sea to the land of promise, a land flowing with milk and honey. It represents the pillar of cloud and fire which guide the children of Israel on their pilgrimage.

Today it is a symbol of Christ which guides the Christian out of bondage to sin and leads us into new life initiated by the reign of the Savior. The light speaks of the resurrection of the Lord and his indwelling power in the baptismal rite; this is the source of our illumination. The baptized become the enlightened ones.[8]

This candle, with all its imagery and meaning, could be intentionally used more often than it is. Other than the font and water itself, it is the most prominent symbol of various meanings of baptism.

The Baptismal Certificate

I have hanging on my wall a beautiful, framed ordination certificate with the bishop's ring embedded upon the melted red wax. Imagine if every bishop put their wax seal on every baptismal certificate! There are a number of ways to enhance and "beautify" the certificate that should remind us of our baptism throughout our lives.

First of all, we could expand all baptismal certificates to a size that was appropriate for framing and hanging in bedrooms, hallways, and offices; this would also ensure that the certificate is large enough for the entire baptismal covenant to appear upon it. Space could be made for parents, godparents, other witnesses, and/or the whole congregation to sign it. This signing can take place in the midst of the service itself or at the reception following.[9] Some might want to display the certificate in the narthex or in the parish hall so that parishioners can sign it, much like what is being done at weddings and funerals today.

Finally, it would be appropriate for the bishop's wax seal and signature to be affixed to the baptismal certificate. This emphasizes both the

---

8. Chapman, "Eight Faces," 67.

9. The signing of the covenant during the service can add to the solemnity of the event and it may also reinforce the commitment made by sponsors and godparents. However, it may come across as looking like a contractual agreement, as well as breaking the flow of the liturgy.

importance of baptism and the connection to the bishop. Certificates could be mailed to the diocesan bishop for their seal and signature ahead of time, which is what I do now. This is one way that we can fulfill the expectation, set by the many prayer books, that baptisms should be tied to the ministry of the bishop. For a final touch, a white ribbon could be placed in the corner of the certificate, as is done with framed diplomas or ordination certificates. I want children to grow up having their baptismal certificate in their bedroom, and possibly in their dorm rooms and offices. Families or even whole congregations could create a "baptism album," with pictures of the event put together, which could include a picture of the certificate along with the vows.

Gifts and Baptism Anniversaries

Congregations could consider publishing baptism anniversary dates rather than (or in addition) to birthdays, and they could be mentioned in the Prayers of the People. Imagine a congregation so in tune with the values and importance of baptism that not only do they send a card on the first anniversary of a person's baptism, but they send it out on the second and third and fourth anniversary, "till death do them part." Each card could contain a reminder of one of the baptismal vows or some other teaching moment. *Imagine growing up and moving around the country, knowing that the congregation who took responsibility for your spiritual life has tracked you as well or better than your alma mater.*[10]

The names of those to be baptized could be published each week in the bulletin during the season in which the baptism is to take place, or at least several weeks before the baptism, like the traditional practice of publishing the banns of marriage several weeks before the wedding. An article about the person and their family would be helpful as well. Additionally, advertising on an outdoor digital sign that a baptism is coming up communicates both to the congregation and the community who drives by.

---

10. On a practical note, our children, youth, and adults in the South are often asked the question, "When were you saved?" I advise people to answer, "Two thousand years ago." However, a nice way of connecting to those asking the question to what they have been constantly reminded of in church, would be to answer, "Well, I was baptized on such and such a date."

Questions for Reflection

1. Imagine from memory, your font, its location, and usage. Then answer the question, "What does that all indicate about baptism or its importance or lack thereof in my parish?" Now go into the sanctuary and discover if what you remember is accurate.

2. Dream up some ideas about how you might enhance the font and candle in its presence, appearance, location, and usage so that it shouts to all who enter this place, "Baptism is important here!"

3. Where is the Paschal candle and when is it lighted? When do you process with it? Are there other liturgical times of year that you could display, light, or process the candle?

4. What does your parish do now/what could they do in the future to connect baptism to the home?

5. How does your congregation celebrate individuals who are baptized, and what else could you do to celebrate?

CHAPTER 8

Preaching and Teaching Moments

Baptism is part of the Church's Proclamation.

Karl Barth[1]

I f you have read this far, you know that to bring baptism to the forefront of your faith tradition involves many parts, from dedicating a season to preaching baptismal themes to rearranging your nave to give the font pride of place. Beyond preaching the right themes at the right time, a speaker or priest has many other opportunities to maximize their oratory for the good of their congregation. The following are further teaching and preaching opportunities to more perfectly proclaim baptismal values within the normal Sunday liturgy, as well as in the liturgy for baptism.[2] Alan Hayes says in his book *Baptism, Historical, Theological and Pastoral Perspectives*, that in the 1549 BCP, Thomas Cranmer had the service for baptism begin with exhortations and teachings: "[Thomas Cranmer] like most Protestants, wanted to be sure that worshippers clearly understood the meaning and intent of every service, ceremony, and sign, since otherwise liturgy had a way of degenerating into a set of meaningless, canned rituals, or even superstition or idolatry."[3]

Preaching sermons on baptism year-round will make a difference, but sometimes actions (*faciendi*—doing) *with* words, speak and preach louder than words alone. David Buttrick, in his book *Homiletic Moves and Structures*, notes how our culture may not value words as much as previous generations, presenting a challenge for preachers who have to deal with

---

1. Karl Barth, *The Teaching of the Church regarding Baptism* (London: S C M Press, 1956), 84.
2. This can even include interrupting the readings to comment on them.
3. Gordon L. Heath and James D. Dvorak, eds., *Baptism, Historical, Theological and Pastoral Perspectives* (Eugene, OR: Pickwick Publications, 2009), 118.

two-minute attention spans.[4] However, it could be good to offer a short word of explanation to go along with actions in the liturgy that reinforce the values of baptism. This is a key element to proclaiming baptism year-round. Fred Craddock, in his preaching classic *As One without Authority*, draws his upside down and right side up triangles regarding induction and deduction in terms of how parishioners/listeners gain insights.[5]

Craddock reminds us to approach preaching from the perspective of the listener, for interrupting readings and parts of the liturgy with preaching moments catches their attention.[6] Parishioners have told me how much more they pay attention to the readings when I interrupt the lector to give some background, or when I interject with a reaction to the reading.

Liturgy is drama, art, formation, teaching, participation, and reenactment. *Preaching can be all these as well.* Taking "preaching moments" throughout the liturgy routinely, or from time to time, can be an effective way to inspire others to seek baptism.[7]

The inductive learning that goes on with these baptismal moments has proven itself in my own parish. I have received consistent positive feedback from parishioners after sprinkling them over and over again at baptismal services and at the renewal of vows. I have heard from some members, "I know I have been sealed by the Holy Spirit in baptism and marked as Christ's own forever!" and "I now understand the vows!"

Once a year, either on one of the four Sundays appointed for baptisms (Easter, Pentecost, All Saints', the Baptism of Our Lord) when there is no baptism, or on an appropriate Sunday sometime during the long season after Pentecost, the presider/celebrant/preacher could walk through the various actions of a baptism, proclaiming the meanings behind them. Presenting an instructed service of Holy Baptism or simply explaining and anticipating baptism on a Sunday or two before a baptism will go a long way in helping the People of God to "dive into" the service when it happens. Just speaking or preaching about it ahead of time reminds the people of the importance the presider puts on baptism. *What speaks more than the words is that the preacher is doing this at all!* It could be that when this

---

4. David Buttrick, *Homiletic, Moves and Structures* (Philadelphia: Fortress Press, 1987), 5–6.

5. Fred B. Craddock, *As One Without Authority* (St. Louis, MO: Chalice Press, 2001), 48.

6. Fred B. Craddock, *Overhearing the Gospel* (St. Louis, MO: Chalice Press, 2002), 103.

7. We just had an hour and forty minute baptismal liturgy on All Saints' Day and that inspired five of the grandchildren of our nursery worker to seek baptism.

is done, no sermon on baptism need be preached on the actual Sunday of the baptism, not to mention that, like Christmas and Easter, the liturgy when enacted well preaches for itself! The bottom line is that we need to explain our liturgies more often so people can understand the full meanings of them.

Marion Hatchett, in referring to universal rites of initiation, says, "The rites, which are invariably spoken of as new birth and as death and resurrection, are designed to make an indelible impression on the initiate and reinforce the impressions of earlier initiations on those who share the ritual."[8] Making an impression on both the congregation and candidates (if old enough) is part and parcel of this ceremony, and preachers and celebrants can do so much more to make that impression.

The following preaching moments would support an instructed service of Holy Baptism or could be worked into a "baptismal sermons series" once every three or so years, preached every Sunday in Lent or in Easter season. These possible preaching moments are written in a personal mode to stimulate through questions the creative thoughts of preachers and those who plan to preach baptism regularly or occasionally.

Liturgical Movement and Outward and Visible Signs Preach and Teach!

Baptismal candidates can process in with the choir and chancel party, and be seated in a place of honor. Children, or perhaps even the entire congregation can process with them. Furniture can be moved to make room for many to gather around the font. Adult baptismal candidates can wear albs (white vestments) to help them stand out in the crowd.

An anthem or psalm can be sung during the procession, or even while the Prayers for the Candidates are being said. Congregations can pause for quiet prayer or a song, such as *Veni Sancte Spiritus*, asking the Holy Spirit to come before the actual act of baptism, as is often done before the act of ordination in ordination services.

During the baptism, candidates should stand facing the congregation rather than the celebrant, so that all are invited to experience and learn from the rite.

---

8. Hatchett, 251.

Invitations, Welcome, and Pomp and Circumstance Preach and Teach!

Baptism is everyone's ordination to ministry, yet we often send out invitations for ordinations but not for baptisms. Many do not even know there is going to be a baptism until they arrive at the service. Do we exert as much energy, pomp, and circumstance around baptisms as we do around ordinations of deacons, priest and bishops or even graduations? What message are we sending about the importance of baptism?

Visual Aids Preach and Teach!

Do we print out the entire baptismal service, as we do at ordinations? There will be visitors to both services who may need guidance. Does the actual act of baptizing have a special place in the bulletin and in the liturgy? Do each of the significant acts—Presentation and Examination, the Baptismal Covenant, the signing of the baptismal certificates with witnesses, Prayers for the Candidates, the baptism, the laying on of hands and anointing, and the welcome—have a significant place of emphasis in the service and bulletin? Do we sing the Prayers for the Candidates, as in ordination services? How do we present the baptismal candles? Has the congregation heard sermons on one or all of these symbolic acts?

The Laying on of Hands Preaches and Teaches!

The laying on of hands, which is part of the Hebrew scriptures and New Testament traditions, often gets lost in the service both in terms of placement in the bulletin and in the service. Does this action, along with the anointing of oil, take place so that the whole congregation can see it? Or does it visually become an addendum to baptism? Does it take place at the font or the altar? Does the preacher preach on these aspects of the ceremony?

Getting Wet Teaches and Preaches!

This is why we are here! Can the whole congregation see, since they are witnesses? Is plenty of water used and allowed to splash onto the floor and over the candidate even if the font is birdbath size? Is the font deep enough that the celebrant can hold an adult's head in the water? The Christian pilgrimage can be messy. It may be a time to mention that immersion is the expected form, since it is listed first in the options listed in the BCP.

Once the water is blessed and the candidate is baptized, how will the congregation participate? We can splash the congregation at either the procession in or after the baptism itself.[9]

Instruction and Teaching Preaches!

Even though parents may actually attend a baptism class before they have their child baptized, there is a good chance that their children will never be catechized, at least until Confirmation, if they attend those classes. Why not "catechize" them every Sunday as they are growing up? Preachers can support the catechumenate, a program for those wanting to be baptized, and the rich rite of baptism by intentionally and appropriately taking opportunities to preach on the symbols, actions, values, history, ethics, sacrament, and theology of baptism. Maxwell Johnson suggests,

> . . . focusing upon life-long post baptismal catechesis [forming disciples] reinforces that for all in the faith community—infants, children, adults—new life begins in initiation and it is to this new life begun in water and the Holy Spirit that all are invited to return constantly for refreshment, renewal, and re-orientation in life.[10]

The Words from Our Liturgical Books Preach and Teach!

"There is one Body and one Spirit . . . "

In the present day and throughout history the Body of Christ has been divided across various denominations, yet we know on a mystical level that God has made us one in the waters of baptism (and in the bread and wine of Eucharist). This is a call to unity through love and respect, as much as it

---

9. One parishioner, after a teaching moment on the sealing with the oil, said to me, "I know I am sealed by the Holy Spirit." Another said regarding being splashed with water, "I think we need to be reminded of our baptisms." I can tell you from these and many other conversations that these kind of preaching moments make a difference.

10. Maxwell E. Johnson, *The Rites of Initiation, Their Evolution and Interpretation* (Collegeville, MN: Liturgical Press, 2007), 465.

is an outward and visible sign of that unity. It is no accident that baptism with water in the name of the Father, Son, and Holy Spirit is recognized by almost all Christian denominations. It is also true that almost all Christians share the experience of being baptized. These unifying words from the liturgy serve as a reminder of Jesus's prayer that we all may be one. *The waters of baptism are thicker than blood and make us one family.*

"I believe!"

The personal pronoun is used as we profess the Apostles' Creed, which echoes many of the earliest professions of faith by those about to be baptized. It is crucial in this age that we all, the newly baptized and the already baptized, know what we believe and what we do not believe. What do we mean when we say, "Jesus is Lord!" in a time in the world when other forces compete to be lord of our lives, whether they be success, consumerism, addiction, political identity, family identity, etc. How will we be able to proclaim Jesus if we do not know what we believe about him?

"I renounce them!"

Each of us must identify the forces of evil in our lives. Some of those can look like a positive influence in our lives, such as the ones mentioned above. The temptation toward hate, judgment, sloth, self-centeredness, snobbery, greed, pride, and those other deadly sins can and will draw us away from Christ.

"We will!"

These are the two most important words uttered at weddings and baptisms. When welcoming the newly baptized, the witnesses and the congregation are committing to provide the prayers, resources, and support for those being baptized, including praying and giving for the spread of the kingdom, giving so there are education programs, and giving so the doors are open for worship for all people. This is about stewardship of the gospel and stewardship of the institutional church.

Not only is the newly baptized incorporated into the Body of Christ, but the Body of Christ is committing to know these persons by name, by personality, by family. This preaching moment could be about the eternal priesthood, and how we are incorporated into the life and ministry of a congregation. Repeating the newly baptized name and sharing something about them would help the congregation to personally, as well as corporately, welcome them. Sharing the names of the parents and godparents would be appropriate.

"And don't you forget it!"

I usually add these words after saying, "You are sealed by the Holy Spirit in Baptism and marked as Christ's own forever!" This is said both after laying on of hands and as water is splashed on the congregation in the procession back to the altar. This is a time to quote Paul in Romans 8, where he says nothing can separate us from the love of God in Christ Jesus!

Rubrics, Instructions, and Exhortations Preach and Teach!

Taking time to reflect and preach upon the rubrics and baptismal instructions from the BCP provides opportunities to further involve the people in the meanings and actions of baptism. Marion Hatchett reminds us in his commentary on the BCP that rubrics and exhortations were at one time read at the church door.[11]

The Call and the Exhortations, which are included in the worship template and are homilies unto themselves, could also be the basis for sermons. The Call is a suggestion on how to begin a service for Holy Baptism from the font before the processional. The Exhortation is a suggested instruction said just before the Presentation of the Candidate. The Call and the Exhortation are for the benefit of the entire congregation, reminding them of what happens in baptism, the theologies underlying baptism, and the recognition that we are all on a lifelong journey of formation. They also are an opportunity for evangelism in terms of the visitors that are usually present at baptisms or for the parents who may be sporadic attendees.

Finally, the Call and Exhortation echo exhortations from the Ash Wednesday service, weddings, and the catechism (BCP, 845). The Call and

---

11. Hatchett, *Commentary of the Book of Common Prayer*, 260.

Exhortations are inspired by excerpts from page 384 of 1989 edition of *The New Zealand Book of Common Prayer* and the Pastoral Introduction in the alternative prayer books for Canada and The Church of England, as well as from some of the original trial liturgies of the American prayer books from the sixties and seventies.[12] The section on quotes from scripture, for those life-long Episcopalians, are borrowed from the format from page 332 in the BCP, reminiscent of the Comfortable Words from the BCP 1928.

Preaching on baptism calls for many supports, including an appropriate catechumenate and a full rite of initiation. However, liturgical actions, the placement of furniture, and the words from the prayer book "preach" quite well. A one-minute homily expounding on any actions in the service may sometimes be more fruitful than a ten-minute sermon on baptism. The more important baptism becomes to the worship leaders and preachers, the more important it will become in liturgical space, words, and action.

Questions for Reflection

1. Which of the above ideas resonate with you? How might you integrate them into your own practices?
2. Would you feel comfortable interrupting the service for a preaching moment? If not, how might you and your fellow worship leaders coordinate to allow for spontaneous interjections for emphasis?

---

12. Shumard, 64.

CHAPTER 9

The History of Baptism

This chapter is added for those who want to further explore the depth of the meanings of baptism, its history, and the history of the rites themselves. It is also included to address those traditionalists who may be saying, "Wait a minute! We cannot change what we are doing! We have always done it that way!"

As we explore the methods of enhancing baptismal values in the liturgy, and thus in our lives, it is crucial that we understand the history of the rites and their interpretations. The current language in the actual rite of baptism, for example, made the news in 2022, as the Roman Catholic Church ruled that baptisms performed by a priest should use the words, "*I baptize* you in the name of the Father, the Son and the Holy Spirit!" rather than the words, "*We baptize* you in the name of the Father, the Son and the Holy Spirit!" Yet the study of history reveals more concern over being baptized in the name of the Trinity than the issue of which pronoun is used. This recent controversy recalls questions of the efficacy of baptism, as well as how the form and language of the rite determine the "validity" of the sacrament.

Let's look at the history of the rites of baptism first. This will give a context for how we approach enhancing the symbols, values, and implications of baptism, Sunday after Sunday.

History of the Theology and Teaching about Baptism

Baptism has been practiced by almost all Christian denominations, which underscores the importance of undergoing the rite. Baptism is part and parcel of professing to be and to practice as Christians. What people through the generations have believed about baptism has ranged far and wide, and the universal church has never been of one mind concerning baptism . . . or much of anything else for that matter!

Dan Edwards, in his commentary on prayer book spirituality, says:

> The rites of Christian Initiation have undergone a long and complex history, with understandings of these rites varying dramatically from time to time and place to place. Conflicts over differing understandings of these rites have been intense and have often represented differing understandings of the very heart of the Christian faith, the nature of the apostolic mission, and the role of the Christian in the social order.[1]

Not surprisingly, many Christians have questions. Is baptism:

- Regeneration, or being born again?
- A washing away of original sin?
- A simple ritual of profession of faith and becoming an official member of the church?
- Being added to the Universal Church of God?
- Influenced by the intent of the one baptized, the sponsors or parents, or the one performing the rite?
- A sacrament or not?

If yes, there's a lot at stake, and getting the exact "formula" is important. If not, not so much.

Some may even wonder: Is baptism even necessary ... for anything? There is scriptural support for baptism being essential to be a Christian, such as the story recorded in Acts 2:37–38, when Peter, filled with the Holy Spirit at Pentecost, converted three thousand people:

> Now when they heard this, they were cut to the heart and said to Peter and the rest of the apostles, "Brothers, what shall we do?" And Peter said to them, "Repent, and be baptized every one of you in the name of Jesus Christ so that your sins may be forgiven: and you will receive the gift of the Holy Spirit."

Yet while on the cross, Jesus himself says to the thief on the cross in Luke 23:33–43, "Today you will be with me in paradise!" Obviously,

---

1. Dan Edwards, *Study Guide to Prayer Book Spirituality* (New York: Church Hymnal Corporation, 1990), 31.

baptism for this person was not a requirement for salvation or a doorway to heaven.

The apostle Paul often refers to baptism as a way to respond to issues within the church. Neither Paul nor any stories mentioned in scripture offer a comprehensive understanding of baptism. In fact, baptism is rarely the primary topic of discussion for Paul. He "uses" the popular experience, in combination with his understanding of baptism, to reinforce other theological or ecclesiological arguments he is making, whether about unity in the church, bad behavior in the church, a call to better behavior in the church, or understanding what Christ has done for the church.

Scripture, tradition, and reason have rarely been consistent, but preachers have the opportunity to clarify this inconsistency. The following are examples of many diverse understandings of baptism.

Many Protestants would think of baptism as primarily a response made by people, yet as the World Council of Churches puts it, "Baptism is both God's gift and our human response to that gift."[2] Many understand baptism simply as the ritual of joining the church or a denomination or as professing an adult belief in Jesus Christ, while still others see it as a sacrament, as something real that causes an inward and spiritual change in the nature of the person and that person's relationship to God.

To sum up much of what Karl Barth says about baptism, "It is all about the work of Jesus, before, during and after baptism more than about what we say or do."[3] Barth believed, "Water-baptism is thus a symbol of the fact we have been redeemed and not itself the means of redemption."[4] His son Markus put it this way, "The ultimate theological point . . . was that Baptism is not an unfailing tool which effects what it portrays, but is to be understood as confession, obedience, hope and prayer."[5]

John Henry Newman, a leader of the nineteenth-century Oxford movement, had a high view of baptism, regarding it as means to salvation, whereas Frederick Maurice, of the Broad Church movement, rejected the

---

2. *Baptism, Eucharist and Ministry*, 25th anniversary printing (Geneva, Switzerland: World Council of Churches, 2010), 3.

3. Karl Barth, *The Teaching of the Church on Baptism* (Great Britain: D. R. Hillman & Sons Press, 1956), 1–25.

4. Spinks, 142.

5. Spinks, 142.

idea that baptism separated the Christian from the ranks of the damned, but was in favor of the sacramental expression of a relationship with Christ, having its basis in creation and the atonement of Christ. To him, baptism expressed a relationship that already existed.[6] In contrast, Richard Hooker, an Anglican writer, took the covenant of baptism as a legal contract, wherein if we did not hold up to our part of the agreement, God would not have to hold up his part.[7]

One important modern articulation of the doctrine of Christian initiation is the Lima Statement of the World Council of Churches, *Baptism, Eucharist and Ministry*, whose four main points are such:

○ Baptism is the complete initiation into the Body of Christ which is the Church.

○ The bond established in Baptism is indissoluble.

○ Confirmation is a renewal rather than a completion of the baptismal covenant.

○ Baptism is unrepeatable, **but should constantly be re-affirmed** during the baptized Christian's "continuing struggle" and "continuing experience of Grace."[8]

Historical theologian John Vissers notes that he is "struck" by the variation of theology and practice surrounding baptism,[9] while Marion Hatchett remarks upon the diversity of theologies expressed in the service of Holy Baptism found in the Book of Common Prayer:

The act was reinterpreted in terms of the Christian Gospel: it meant a cleansing from the blood of Jesus, new birth in Christ, death and resurrection in Christ, incorporation into His Body, the "mark" and "seal" of Christ's Sonship, and His anointing (as kings and priests were anointed), to receive the Holy Spirit, to confess one's faith in Christ, to swear one's loyalty to Him.[10]

---

6. Edwards, 32.
7. Edwards, 33.
8. Edwards, 32–33.
9. Heath and Dvorak, 231.
10. Marion J. Hatchett, *Commentary on the American Prayer Book* (San Francisco: Harper Collins, 1980), 252.

It is important to remember that various theologies behind, beneath, and within Holy Baptism are continually in orbit around one another. This is true both within denominations and in the minds of Jesus's followers, past, present, and future.

Mr. Vissers notes the interdependence and interactions among denominations considering the theology and practice of baptism. Some theologies of baptism, as in so many theological arguments, are emphasized in contrast to other theologians or denominations, such as when defending adult baptism only, over and against infant baptisms. These theologies are still evolving.

Bryan Spinks notes that there are many crosscurrents within current church history:

> The latter half of the twentieth century has been a time of considerable ecumenical activity. Theologians have tended to write for an ecumenical audience or have sought to bring their denomination and tradition into dialogue with other denominations and traditions, seeking areas of agreement as well as pointing out areas of disagreement.[11]

Most of these historical understandings of baptism can be identified in the service for Holy Baptism in the BCP, especially within the prayer of Thanksgiving over the Water on pages 306–307:

> We thank you Father, for the water of Baptism. In it we are buried with Christ in his death. By it we share in his resurrection. Through it we are reborn of the Holy Spirit. Therefore in joyful obedience to your Son, we bring into his fellowship those who come to him in faith, baptizing them in the name of the Father, and of the Son, and of the Holy Spirit.
>
> Now sanctify this water, we pray you, by the power of your Holy Spirit, that those who here are cleansed from sin and born again may continue for ever in the risen life of Jesus Christ our Savior.

The service, like Paul's treatment of baptism, provides opportunities to reflect upon our beliefs, not just about baptism, but concerning the work of

---

11. Spinks, 137.

Jesus Christ as reflected in the Apostles' Creed. The baptismal vows echo Paul's taking the opportunity to speak about the ethics of baptism and life in Christ.

Ruth Meyers, referring to the indissolubility of baptism and Paul's experience of Christ living in him, summarizes the theologies contained within the sacrament of baptism in the BCP:

> We who are many have become one Body of Christ. We who were not a people have become God's people. We who have been buried with Christ in his death have been made partakers of his risen life. We who have died to sin have been raised to new life in the Holy Spirit. By uniting us to himself, the Great High Priest and King of kings, ordains us to the royal priesthood of all believers and fills us with the Holy Spirit, forgives our sins, gives us a share in his new life in the communion of saints (the one holy, catholic and apostolic Church), sends us into the world in mission and looks forward to the day of redemption.[12]

The history of debates surrounding baptism demonstrates a continued interest in the following questions:

- Does the act impart grace?
- Is the act only a sign of grace?
- What does it mean to die with Christ in baptism and be raised with Christ in this life now?
- When does the Holy Spirit come into a person's life?
- Does the bishop's laying on of hands and anointing impart grace or indicate grace, impart the Holy Spirit or confirm the Spirit?
- When are our sins washed away and how often?
- Is there such a thing as original sin?
- Should baptism wait until the child is old enough to understand?

These are questions still being debated, so I will not enter into the fray with my own answers. However, it is important that preachers are clear

---

12. Ruth Meyers and Leonel Mitchell, *Praying Shapes Believing, A Theological Commentary on The Book of Common Prayer* (New York: Seabury Press, 2016), 102.

about their own understanding of baptism, or at least know the arguments for each. These questions will likely be on the minds of many of their parishioners.

Historical Perceptions from Scripture

As we consider adding to our liturgies, it is important that we look at how scripture historically views baptism. Despite the historical disagreements about theologies of baptism within the theological communities and within Christendom itself, it does not appear that baptism or the theologies reflected in it were controversial within scripture. A mutual understanding of baptism often appears to be presumed by the writers of the New Testament. The people of the time witnessed so many baptisms that Paul assumes his readers agree with him about baptism, using familiar imagery and theology behind baptism to make a point, such as the images of being clothed with a white robe as it relates to being clothed with Christ, or that people who saw catechumens go under the water and come out would connect this to images of dying and rising to new life. Still, no discussion on the theologies of baptism could take place without looking more deeply into a few classical pieces of scripture that relate to Paul's themes in baptism: dying and rising with Christ, finding unity in Christ through baptism, putting on Christ and being baptized in the name of Christ and not in the name of another person.

Paul, in Romans, speaks of dying and rising with Christ. We typically read this passage during the Easter Vigil, but it would be good to review at all baptisms!

> What then are we to say? Should we continue to sin in order that grace abound? By no means! How can we who died to sin go on living in it? Do you not know that all of us who have been baptized into Christ Jesus were baptized into his death? Therefore, we have been buried with him by Baptism into death, so that just as Christ was raised from the dead by the glory of the Father, so we too might walk in newness of life. For if we have been united with him in a death like his, we will certainly be united with him in a resurrection like his. We know that our old self was crucified with

him so that the body of sin might be destroyed, and we might no longer be enslaved to sin.

Paul's Letter to the Romans 6:1–6

Paul explains how going under the waters of baptism is like dying with Christ on the cross and coming out of the waters is like rising with Christ, and so in some ways what happened on the cross happens to us (see Colossians 2: 8–15[13] and 1 Timothy 2.11–12). Paul is attempting to lead his readers and listeners into understanding that they need to let go of (let die) their old ways, and live lives worthy of the sacrifice Jesus made.

Paul also wants to reinforce to Gentiles that they have been born again as legal heirs, along with those of Hebrew descent, to all the rights and privileges of being born a Jew, but without all the rites and legalism. Paul, as usual, is not teaching about baptism, but rather using the "sacrament" to urge his readers to live lives worthy of baptism.

Paul—known as Saul before his conversion—of course was using his own spiritual experience of letting "die" his zealousness for the Pharisaic ways and dying and rising to live the "zealous" way of Jesus, the way of the cross, the way of a new beginning. Paul is often encouraging the Gentile converts to give up their old "pagan" ways, though for Paul, I can imagine in his own mind and in his own experience of combatting the "Judaizers," that he had to let go of/exchange his legalistic ways for the grace of God. Like Martin Luther, this experience most likely colored a major part of Paul's theology and almost all his teaching upon baptism.

Nicholas Taylor, in his book on Paul and baptism, states:

> . . . theologically, baptism into the death of Christ continues to affect our lives. A mystical connection between going under the water equates with the death of Jesus on the cross. We don't have to be crucified or take up our cross, for in the waters of baptism we are crucified with Christ. We identify with Christ's death in baptism; and the death of Christ on the cross is actualized in the waters of baptism.[14]

---

13. Paul's authorship is questioned here, though it fits with Pauline thought.
14. Nicholas Taylor, *Paul on Baptism: The Theology, Mission and Ministry in Context* (London: SCM Press, 2016), 43.

Speaking pastorally, being transformed as Saul-to-Paul was, dying and rising with Christ, is probably a difficult concept for those who have not had a "born again" experience or previously held an understanding of their spiritual lives as a journey of death and rebirth. We live in a culture of "finding oneself" and building one's own kingdoms, rather than finding ourselves in Christ and losing ourselves, our very lives, for the sake of the kingdom of God.

Theologically speaking, our God chose the way of living, loving, dying, and rising as God's way to engage us in redemption. There are echoes of this sacrificial living and dying throughout scripture, including the story of the sacrifice of Isaac, the images of Noah and the flood, and Exodus. The themes of death and resurrection echo not only through the above stories, but through other readings at the Easter Vigil (BCP, 288–292), as well as the prayer of Thanksgiving over the Water of baptism (BCP, 306–307).

Paul speaks of us finding our unity and common inheritance in Christ Jesus in baptism and the imagery of baptism.

> Just as the body is one and has many members, and all the members of the body, though many, are one body, so it is with Christ. For in the one Spirit we were all baptized into the one Body—Jews or Greeks, slaves or free—and we were all made to drink one Spirit. Indeed the body does not consist of one member but of many.
>
> *1 Corinthians 12:12–14*

> Therefore the law was our disciplinarian until Christ came, so that we might be reckoned as righteous by faith. But now that faith has come, we are no longer subject to a disciplinarian, for in Christ Jesus you are all children of God through faith. As many of you were baptized in Christ have clothed yourselves with Christ. There is no longer Jew or Greek, there is no longer slave or free, there is no longer male or female; for all of you are one in Christ Jesus.
>
> *Galatians 3:23–28*

Paul is speaking of the workings and ministries of the church; connecting them to baptism in Christ; and reminding all that we find our unity, our humility, and our exaltation in the waters of baptism and the work of Jesus Christ. We become one body in baptism, realizing that *water is thicker than blood* when it comes to ethnic, social, racial, economic, and political parts of the Body. Paul often recalls our unity found in baptism and reminds his readers that baptism calls us to unity in Christ Jesus.

In Galatians, Paul is—there is no other way to put it—angry, or at least miffed at some Christians. Paul uses foul language when he says of the legalists who thought a Christian had to become a Jew and be circumcised that he wished the knife would slip and they castrate themselves. He also called them "sons of dogs." Once again, Paul brings baptism into an argument about something other than baptism. Paul is in the midst of reminding his readers that they have received the promise of Abraham through faith and that they are all one in Christ. He is reassuring them that in their baptism, they were incorporated into the family of Abraham, legal heirs to the promises of God. Paul writes earlier, "You foolish Galatians! The only thing I want to learn from you is this: Did you receive the Spirit by observing the law?" It sounds like people were tempted to return to the law and needed convincing by Paul. Sometimes I think Christians are tempted to return to the laws of the Hebrew scriptures, and we preachers have to remind them of God's grace.

Despite his frustrations, Paul continues to make a case for faith versus working to keep the law. Paul knows it failed him as a Pharisee. The law was a custodian until Jesus came. Paul is using baptism to prove a point rather than preaching on baptism. We are baptized into Christ! You have clothed yourself with Christ! There is neither Jew or Greek, male or female, free or slave! There are no social or genetic distinctions. We are all legal heirs of Abraham.

We can speak on inclusiveness in so many of the New Testament writings, such as the two quotes above and in stories in Acts. Peter says in the household of Cornelius, "Can anyone withhold the water for baptizing these people who have received the Holy Spirit just as we have? And he commanded them to be baptized in the name of Jesus Christ" (Acts 10:47).

Some see the fact that Peter baptized Cornelius's entire household as support for infant baptism. The real theme is about inclusiveness in the midst of a strong mindset of exclusivity and the rigorous ritual demands of the community. Peter of course asks this question rhetorically, because in fact he knows he will be questioned and criticized, not just by misled believers, but by the leaders of the institution. Not only was Peter worried about having witnesses, but the writer of the Gospel wanted to make clear this was the work of God and not Peter. Once again, in scripture baptism is intimately connected with the coming of the Spirit, and the Spirit works as it pleases and is not confined to institutional sacraments.

This scripture around baptism certainly applies to our lives and debates of the day. Who is in and who is out? Who are the first-class Christians and the nominal Christians? Are we living values reflected in being baptized into Christ? Are we going to accept as equal members to the party anyone who is significantly different from those in power?

This can all be tied into this not-so-original conflict in Acts and the early church, when Christians were already asking whether to accept back into the church those who renounced Jesus to save their lives in light of persecution, or wondering whether baptisms and ordinations were valid in light of personal sin or heresy?

Similar questions have been asked in modern times, seen in the debates around ordaining Gene Robinson, an openly gay bishop. Christians today asked, "Is the ordination of a gay bishop valid? Are sacraments that he or she preside at, valid?" Similarly, some people still wonder whether divorced and remarried people are to be full members of the one holy catholic and apostolic church. Scripture and ongoing church history leans in favor of inclusivity, yet always, it seems, with a fight.

This would not surprise Paul, who was always in a fight about such things in the church, always jostling, alongside the original apostles, for power and connection, even as they walked along the way with Jesus.

Yet baptism is a symbol of and a call to unity—a demand that our divisions cease. No political theological parties, evangelicals, progressives, liberals, fundamentalists, and so on, should separate us from the love of God in Christ. There is one faith, one baptism, one hope and call. God calls us to unity of purpose, unity of identity, unity of theology. Paul calls upon our common experience of baptism to lead us from discord to unity, and from bad behavior to good behavior. You were baptized in the name of Jesus, not Paul, and baptism does not depend upon the theology of the church or person who baptized you.

Finally, one doctrine or belief that most, if not all, Christian denominations would agree on about baptism, despite the diversity of beliefs, is that the newly baptized are incorporated into the church and/or into the greater "universal and apostolic" church of Christ. The congregation also takes responsibility for nurturing the faith of the newly baptized. These two aspects of initiation into the church are fairly common among denominations and support the lifelong journey of the baptized.

Baptism and the End Times

Finally, baptism has an eschatological aspect, even as it is performed in the present while reflecting the past. The words from the Sunday Eucharist reflect the reality of Christ's work, which is ours to discover in baptism as well as Eucharist: *Christ has died. Christ has risen. Christ will come again.* Laurence Stookey remarks, "Baptism pushes us into the future, even as it helps us to understand the tradition of the Church and to live as contemporary disciples."[15] The sacraments of baptism and Eucharist reflect both realized and anticipated eschatology—the work of Jesus Christ, past, present and future.

Susan Wood clarifies this as she explores the ecumenical dimensions of the doctrines of baptism:

> Sacraments memorialize the past and anticipate the future within present symbolic events and symbolic time, concentrating past and future within a present event. Within the ritual time of the liturgy, past and future are gathered into the present moment through memorial, presence and anticipation. Thus, in baptism, when we participate in the death and resurrection of Christ, these past events are brought into the present. When we rise sacramentally to new life with Christ and participate in the new creation, the fullness of that new life and new creation still await us in the eschaton.[16]

The above quote reminds me of a spiritual experience I undergo so often when performing a baptism or celebrating Eucharist. *I sense that the past, present and future merge at that moment* (we call that Kairos time,

---

15. Laurence Hall Stookey, *Baptism, Christ's Art in the Church* (Nashville: Abingdon, 1982), 16.
16. Susan K. Wood, *One Baptism, Ecumenical Dimensions of the Doctrine of Baptism* (Collegeville, MN: Liturgical Press), 2009.

a moment of indeterminate time), and I stand with all the baptized in the universe, past, present and future, as we usher in the newest child of God.

The sacrament itself may reflect all the theologies and doctrines, while holding them both firmly and lightly and in tension with one another. We would do well to hold our own theology of baptism lightly. Some doctrines are to be pondered, meditated and chewed upon, rather than codified, inflicted, or spewed upon others.

Liturgy, the People of God, Clergy and Traditions

Liturgy, at its best, comes through the hands of professionals, but is also the natural expression of the people of God. So, when we plan our liturgies, let us take the best of the past, heed the critical voices of the present, and embrace the imagination of visionaries; we can mix them all into the lives of the people of God, the baptized.

We have the freedom as well as the responsibility to take both history and our contemporary experiences seriously. When something in church history has been debated for the entire sweep of history, we might choose to be both humbled and inspired enough to have the courage to form our own statements and beliefs, while recognizing that they too will change. For example, in The Episcopal Church we now ordain women, and divorce, and remarriage is no longer an impediment to receiving communion. After all, with Paul, we see through a glass darkly and we make our best choices, which may be right or wrong, good, or bad.

This book is not designed to defend one theological, historical, traditional, or symbolic view of baptism over the other. The key point is to take baptism and its symbols and values seriously, through continuous reinforcement, allowing it to be consciously and unconsciously absorbed into our souls.

History of the Book of Common Prayer:
A Context For Change

This section is addressed more to traditionalists who think change is a bad word. Okay, let's not use the word "change." Maybe you have heard the jokes:

"How many Presbyterians (or Methodists, or Episcopalians) does it take to change a light bulb?"

"Change?! My great grandfather gave that light bulb!"

Another answer might be, "Five! One to change the light bulb and a memorial committee to talk about how great the previous light bulb was."

I tend to use the word "perfecting" rather than changing. Each generation adds to what the previous has offered, which means we are all perfecting the liturgy. This is the primary purpose of the prayer book.

One reason I go into such detail about the history of the Book of Common Prayer and its many revisions is because I recommend some revisions to the liturgy in this book. Many traditional Episcopalians—and this may be true for other denominational members as well—may say, "We have always done it this way." Knowing the history of the prayer book demonstrates that we were born out of change and have been revising the prayer book and the liturgy throughout the generations. The liturgy will never be *perfect*, but along with Thomas Cranmer, who wrote the original English prayer book in the sixteenth century, and those who have revised prayer books through the generations, let us move toward perfection.

Many denominations have either modeled or taken excerpts from the Anglican and Episcopal prayer books. Exploring the history of some of these books will help us find ways to enhance our liturgies, regardless of denomination. Our current prayer book in The Episcopal Church was also influenced by the ecumenical group of liturgical scholars who in the 1960s worked on the liturgy for Holy Eucharist that emerged from the Roman Catholic Church's Vatican II Conference. Therefore the two current liturgies are quite similar. These scholars closely examined the liturgies of the Western church in the first few hundred years of Christianity. History matters! There is a significant ecumenical nature to the liturgy found in our prayer book. We need to understand these books and those who shaped them so that any suggestions offered will be congruent with the traditions.

The Book of Common Prayer was written during the Reformation by the sixteenth-century reformer Thomas Cranmer, the archbishop of Canterbury in The Church of England. His book incorporated the

Latin (Roman Catholic) tradition into a significantly different expression of the liturgy, creating for the people something both familiar and strange. Cranmer translated old Latin prayers into the vernacular, created new prayers, and included ancient prayers and practices from the early churches. He eliminated some of what critics of Rome called the medieval "hocus pocus" practices, which had evolved through the Middle Ages into the Roman liturgy. This first 1549 Book of Common Prayer met great resistance: blood, sweat and tears were spilled because of it. It was radically revised in 1552 and then slightly revised in 1559, 1604, and 1662. The Book of Common Prayer has also been adapted and revised several times in the United States and in Anglican Provinces around the world.

The 1662 Book of Common Prayer is still the official version in England, though most congregations use *Common Worship*, an alternative prayer book published in England in Advent of 2000, somewhat modeled after the Episcopal prayer book. One can find some of the same prayers in the books from several mainline denominations. The late Dean William Palmer Ladd of the Berkley Divinity School wrote in 1941 and in a somewhat self-congratulatory tone:

> Our *Book of Common Prayer* is the best in the world. For four centuries it has exercised an invaluable influence for good throughout the English-speaking world. To find fault with it is an ungracious task. Yet we must remember that its great virtue is due to the fact that originally it was an adaptation of older services to the needs of its own day. That adaptation was made 390 years ago. Since then, the world has changed. Controversies that influenced the old compilers and revisers are now dead. The needs of the twentieth century are not those of the sixteenth. And liturgical science has made enormous progress, even in the last twenty-five years. The time for reconsideration is ripe.[17]

The Book of Common Prayer has been what Anglicans hold not only in common, but what they keep in their hands, hearts, and minds. It is considered so important to Episcopalians that we are renowned, rightly

---

17. Mitchell, *Liturgical Change*, 5.

or wrongly, for knowing the prayer book far better than we know Holy Scriptures. We have parishioners who insist that the entire service *not* be put into a bulletin so that everyone will have to pick up the physical book and use it.[18] It is no wonder that the revision of the Book of Common Prayer (1928) took decades of research and preparation. The approval of the new prayer book, at least until recent times, created the most emotionally divisive event in the life of The Episcopal Church since the American Revolution.

This latest revision was written in the same spirit of Thomas Cranmer, for it too incorporated the ancient traditions into significantly different expressions of the liturgy. Those who formed this new prayer book translated old Elizabethan English prayers into the vernacular, created new prayers, and included more ancient prayers and practices from the early churches. They also borrowed from the most recent scholarship in the Roman Catholic Church, the Lutheran Church, and many ecumenical liturgical scholars. *Full participation by the laity in the liturgy and in ministry was a crucial part of the revisions, and the new prayer book communicated a more celebrative tone than the previous more penitential-oriented prayer book.* Dr. Leonel Mitchell said in his commentary on the 1979 prayer book, *Praying Shapes Believing*:

> The revision of the Prayer Book was more for us than simply the alteration of a service book. It called for a readjustment of the language of our relationship with God and therefore affected that relationship itself. Traditionally this dependence of theology upon worship has been expressed in the Latin maxim, *lex orandi, lex credendi*—that the way we pray determines the way we believe.[19]

It is no wonder that the Standing Liturgical Commission of The Episcopal Church drew upon the expertise and advice of so many traditional and progressive liturgical scholars, and those who embodied both. They worked on these revisions for decades in the twentieth century. This group consisted of bishops, scholars, priests, and even the famous

---

18. This was true in the parish where I was recently rector and I have heard similar tales from other rectors.

19. Mitchell, *Praying Shapes Believing, A Theological Commentary on the Book of Common Prayer* (Chicago: Winston Press, 1985), 1.

anthropologist Margaret Mead.[20] All of this is to say that whatever liturgical enhancements or supplements to the liturgy are offered here are done in fear and trembling, and with a fervent desire to be congruent with the current BCP.

The Book of Common Prayer and the church universal have always lifted up the sacraments of Holy Baptism and Holy Communion as crucial to our life together. The current Book of Common Prayer clearly puts them at the core of our liturgical life. One rite follows the other in the layout of the book.

However, both have ebbed and flowed in importance throughout the generations. We see in this current prayer book the continuation of change in line with the Liturgical Renewal Movement, which had been emerging since the late nineteenth century and that began in the Roman Catholic Church. There was a desire to reconnect to the past, involve the laity, and improve the quality of the liturgy. Octave Beauduin, an original leader of the Liturgical Movement of Mont Cesar, said that the liturgy must be democratized.[21] Pope Pius XI, in the early twentieth century, instituted more chants, encouraged children to take communion, and ordered that communion be offered to the laity more often. He also improved the lectionary and had the regular Sunday Eucharist readings take precedence over many saint's days.[22] Vatican II breathed fresh air into the Liturgical Movement in the 1960s, especially into the initiation rites with the adult catechumenate program (RCIA—Rite of Christian Initiation for Adults). The revisers of our prayer book inherited this spirit of revision that was in fact springing forth all over the world. There was dialogue and mutual sharing of resources among scholars of many denominations. This particular group of revisionists, like Cranmer before them, made some serious changes in the 1928 prayer book that created significant readjustments to the way the people in the pews engaged "church," one another, and God.

The structure of the Book of Common Prayer itself sets the stage for the relationship of Holy Baptism and Holy Communion by the very placement of each in the book. The service of Holy Baptism concludes

---

20. Leonel Mitchell, a draft memoir emailed to the author (Chicago, January 3, 2009).
21. Geoffrey Wainwright and Karen Westerfield Tucker, eds., *The Oxford Dictionary of Christian Worship* (New York: Oxford University Press, 2006), 696–697.
22. Ibid.

on page 314 of the BCP and is immediately followed with the service for Holy Eucharist, which begins on page 315. There is a vibrant liturgical connection that ties the table and font together. Almost all the Christian denominations hold to baptism and Holy Communion as the two primary sacraments of the church. Jeffrey Lee states in the church's teaching series on the BCP, "At the heart of *The Book of Common Prayer* stands the liturgical celebration of Christ's death and resurrection—the Paschal mystery—and our participation in that mystery through Baptism and Eucharist."[23] Michael Moriarty commented in his article on W. Palmer Ladd, a participant in the revisions:

> The 1979 *BCP* recognized that fundamental sociological changes had altered the relation of the Church to the surrounding world. It explicitly provided for the liturgical priesthood of the laity, recognized the Eucharist as the principle act of Christian worship on the Lord's Day and articulated the social consequences of Eucharist and Baptism for a Church no longer coterminous with society, which must be intentional in making disciples.[24]

Many of us remember when baptisms were a private affair just with priest and family present. This changed with the new prayer book. The Standing Liturgical Commission, in *Prayer Book Studies 18*, reflected on the call contained in baptism:

> The intent of the (baptismal) liturgy as proposed is that it shall be celebrated at the main Sunday Service several times a year, with the whole congregation joining in the baptismal promises. It is designed to express the corporate faith with which the candidates for Baptism are united and to allow every person present, explicitly to renew their own commitments and to enable the fellowship to recognize its responsibility to the candidates. Since Baptism is here associated directly with the Holy Communion, that sacrament will come to be understood, even on other occasions, as an opportunity

---

23. Jeffrey Lee, *The New Church's Teaching Series*, vol. 7: *Opening the Prayer Book* (Cambridge: Cowley Publications, 1999), 85.

24. Christopher Irvine, ed., *They Shaped Our Worship* (London: Society for Promoting Christian Knowledge, 1998), 63.

for the personal and corporate commitment, self-oblation and reconsecration to Christ.[25]

A number of changes in the regular Sunday worship service came about as both a direct and indirect result of these revisions to the prayer book.

1. Baptism was expected to be initiation into the full membership and life of the church, which included immediate access to Holy Communion. (Previously, confirmation was the doorway to receiving Holy Communion.)

2. Holy Baptism takes place in the context of the regular Sunday Eucharist. This was a shift from the practice of private baptisms.

3. The bishop was expected to preside at baptisms—though they rarely do today.

4. The anointing with oil, the laying on of hands, and the prayer for the Holy Spirit was to take place at baptism.

5. The new prayer book attempted to make clear that the holy people of God were clergy and people gathered together, whereas the previous structure of worship could give the impression that all the "holy actions and people" were located beyond the altar rails.

6. The new prayer book *remembered* the ministry of the baptized, the priesthood of all believers, which both clergy and people share and these principles apply to almost all Christian denominations. This understanding was acted out in the liturgy by what was spelled out in the catechism found in the back of the prayer book, pages 855–856:

Q. Who are the ministers of the Church?
*A. **The ministers of the Church are lay persons, bishops, priests and deacons.***

Q. What is the ministry of the laity?
*A. **The ministry of lay persons is to represent Christ and his Church; to bear witness to him wherever they may be; and according to the gifts given them, to carry on Christ's work of reconciliation in the world; and to take their place in the life, worship, and governance of the Church.***

---

25. *Prayer Book Studies 18*, "Holy Baptism and the Laying on of Hands" (New York: Church Pension Fund), 18.

Q. What is the duty of all Christians?

*A. **The duty of all Christians is to follow Christ; to come together week by week for corporate worship; and to work, pray, and give for the spread of the kingdom of God.***

The service of Holy Baptism in the *Book of Common Prayer* expresses Paul's understanding that we are drowned (buried) with Christ in the waters of baptism and raised from those waters to new life, born again, and anointed by the Holy Spirit for ministry. Once we were dead. Now we are alive. The following quotes from Paul capture part of these meanings and might be appropriate readings for baptisms today. They are words of radical liberation and inclusiveness:

As many of you were baptized into Christ have clothed yourselves with Christ. There is no longer Jew and Greek, there is no longer slave or free, there is no longer male or female; for all of you are one in Christ Jesus . . . And because you are children, God has sent forth the Spirit of His Son into our hearts, crying "Abba! Father!"

Galatians 3:27–28; 4:6

"So if anyone is in Christ, there is a new creation; everything old has passed away; see everything has become new!"

2 Corinthians 5:17

Cyril of Jerusalem said to those who had just been baptized:

In one and the same action you died and were born; the water of salvation became both tomb and womb (mother) for you. What Solomon said of others is apposite to you. On that occasion he said, "There is a time to be born and a time to die," but the opposite is true in your case—there is a time to die and a time to be born. A single moment achieves both ends, and your begetting was simultaneous with your death.[26]

---

26. Johnson, *The Rites*, 96.

Questions for Reflection

1. What did you learn from this chapter that you did not already know?
2. What if anything would you like to change, delete, or add to the rite of baptism as you know it?

CHAPTER 10

Conclusion

Preaching baptism regularly from season to season, year to year, and generation to generation is essential for the lifelong spiritual formation and journey of the entire congregation. No catechumenate program, baptismal sermon at a baptism, recitation of the baptismal vows, or prominent positioning of the baptismal font will by themselves fulfill the need for congregational transformation through baptismal formation, but doing all of the above will. Even a few small steps or words could make a world of difference to people's understanding of the values of baptism, and the way they live their lives.

I hope and pray I have provided enough steps to spark your imagination for accelerating the pace at which baptismal values are incorporated into the spiritual journey. The transformation of the congregation will accelerate because we are:

- Preaching baptism throughout the years
- Routinely reciting the vows
- Seasonally renewing the vows
- Performing liturgical acts in large and visible ways
- Making actual baptisms a big celebratory event
- Arranging the furniture to highlight baptism
- Interrupting parts of the service for preaching moments about baptism
- And regularly splashing the people!

The Book of Common Prayer allows for, and some would say encourages, flexibility and creativity for those who plan worship, and I pray you will follow its direction, even though it could mean a major paradigm "adjustment" for both the clergy and the people. To truly fully embrace baptism one must be willing to ask for more time and energy from both parishioners and clergy. Think about it as helping our people pack their bags for the long baptismal journey!

Preaching baptism year-round adds to the power of the sacrament itself, which has its own authority, integrity, and place. This reinforces the Sundays appointed in the Book of Common Prayer for renewing baptismal vows, for each of these Sundays makes up a unique piece of the tapestry of baptismal theology and experience. Preaching baptism year-round in the majority of churches that have a small Sunday attendance—and thus few baptisms—gives the opportunity to expand upon baptismal meanings and values in ways that would never happen if sermons on baptism were only delivered when there was to be a baptism. Preaching the vows year-round reinforces the ethical life of a Christian, offering context for our intended behaviors.

Let us preach baptism well beyond the normal recommended Sundays. Let us preach baptism well beyond the day of a baptism. Let us preach on the history of baptism! Let us preach baptism by water, word, fire, and Spirit! Let us preach the power of the Holy Spirit!

Let us preach the depth and breadth of all that baptism is:

- A lifelong journey of dying and rising with Christ!
- A letting go of the desires of this world!
- A living out the priesthood of all believers!
- Being empowered by the Holy Spirit for mission and ministry!
- A new birth!
- Being incorporated into the one holy catholic and apostolic church with all rights, privileges, and responsibilities!

Let us continue in the apostles' teaching and fellowship by the breaking of bread and the prayers, by renouncing evil and temptation in all its forms, by repenting and *turning and returning* to the Lord over and over again; by proclaiming by word and deed the gospel of Jesus Christ; by seeking and serving Christ in others, loving our neighbors as ourselves; and by striving for peace and justice, respecting the dignity of every human being.

And finally, let us continually preach baptismal values throughout our lifetime, reminding our people that we have been sealed by the Holy Spirit in baptism and marked as Christ own forever!

Appendix A
The Question of Open Communion

Within the first three hundred years of Christianity, baptism and communion were intimately connected and baptism, more often than not, was the doorway to receiving Holy Communion. In many churches, those preparing for baptism, were dismissed before Holy Communion, and only admitted after their instruction time was over and they were baptized. This may have had to do with the danger of becoming a Christian at the time. Let us remember that there has never been total agreement on the theology of or practice of baptism. There is room for discussion.

The 2022 General Convention of the Episcopal Church was considering a proposed resolution to do away with the requirement of being baptized as a condition for one receiving Holy Communion. It did not make it to a vote. I believe we should encourage and expect baptism and Holy Communion as intimate partners in fully participating in the life of the church. However, things have changed since the first few hundred years of Christianity, and now all are invited to church. Refusing to offer Holy Communion to all is like inviting people to dinner but only giving them appetizers.

Offering Holy Communion to those who have not yet been baptized is out of order, but not beyond scriptural precedent. Scripture reveals that there are exceptions to the normal order of things. Jesus said to the criminal on the cross, who had not been baptized and had not taken communion, "Today you will be with me in paradise!" Peter, whose sermon was interrupted by the falling of the Holy Spirit upon unbaptized and uncircumcised Gentiles at Cornelius's household, said, "The Holy Spirit has come upon these Gentiles as it came upon us. Who can forbid baptism to them?" He got in some trouble with the "General Convention" in Jerusalem, but had plenty of witnesses and he won the day. Paul encountered some disciples who had been baptized but not received the Holy Spirit, and he laid his hands on them and they did receive the Holy Spirit. It appears, as Jesus said, "The Holy Spirit blows where it wills!" We cannot control the Holy

Spirit as much as the institution of the church attempts to do so! Let us remember that Jesus gave communion to Judas who betrayed him, Peter who denied him, and all his apostles who deserted him! None of them truly understood what Jesus was offering.

I have shared in this book that I answer yes to anyone who wants to be baptized recognizing it is a life-long journey. Likewise, I would not refuse communion to anyone asking for it, though I would encourage all who want to fully participate in the Christian life to be baptized, and regularly take communion.

Appendix B
Sample Baptismal Sermons

The Book of Common Prayer recommends that baptisms or the Renewal of Baptismal Vows be done on the feasts of Easter, Pentecost, All Saints' Day, and the Baptism of Our Lord, and when the bishop visits. The following four sermons are meant to stimulate ideas for the four feast days, especially when there is no baptism.

The themes from these feast days can cover most of the theological and sacramental aspects of baptism and this is the advantage of preaching them when there are no baptisms. Preaching these four Sundays alone, even if no other sermons were preached on a different Sunday, would constitute preaching baptism year-round.

I have written these to be preached in an Episcopal Church setting, but they still offer ideas for use in other denominations. Sermons are written in the style in which I preach, including grammar variations. There is more within each sermon than what is actually delivered, not only because that is the usual way I write and then give sermons, but because I have added more as potential resources for preachers.

Easter

"Alleluia the Lord is Risen! Uh-oh!"
An Easter sermon to be preached when there are no baptisms.

Easter is about shock and awe and fear and wonder ... with just an inkling of belief in the resurrection and its implications. Easter is also about "Uh-oh!" What does this mean ... for me ... for you ... for the church and the world?" Paul speaks to the meaning of Easter and especially its meaning for baptism. He would say that Easter is about dying and rising with Christ on the cross, in the grave and empty tomb.

One aspect of baptism that Paul envisions, experiences, and writes about, is being buried in the waters of baptism with Christ and rising with Christ out of the waters to a new life, where we clothe ourselves with

Christ, becoming part of the Body of Christ. The font becomes both tomb and womb. Cyril of Jerusalem, in the fourth century, puts it this way as he reminds those who had already been baptized, which includes most of us in this room . . .

> Ye were led to the Holy Pool of Baptism as Christ was carried from the cross to the Sepulcher . . . [Ye] descended three times into the water and ascended again; here also hinting by a symbol at the three days burial of Christ . . . And at the self-same moment ye were both dying and being born; and that Water of salvation was at once your grave and your mother."[1]

What *of* us or *in* us must die to be born again? I cannot answer for you. I can answer for me as a priest, pastor, and preacher. It is one thing to be born again in a dramatic spiritual way and yet I have noticed in my life that new deaths and new births can happen repeatedly. I noted the other day when I preached the evening of Ash Wednesday, when I was exhausted from the varied activities I participated in during the day, that I did not feel that I brought much energy to the evening sermon. I received however, many positive responses to the sermon in that it had an impact on their spiritual lives. Could it be that my exhaustion allowed my extroverted persona to "die" in order that Christ might be better preached? (Note the First Corinthians reading in the Daily Office, Year Two, I Lent, Monday, where Paul speaks of not preaching himself and preaches the gospel without overwhelming listeners with intellectual wisdom.) Baptism reminds us that we preachers must especially be willing to let many things die within ourselves (over and over again?) in order to let Christ shine through us.

We preachers must explore answering this question (What must die?), maybe before we preach on it. Letting my defenses down allowed more space for the Holy Spirit to speak through me. So often we preachers . . . okay, let me make an "I" statement here! So often" I" can see where letting things die; letting go of my agenda, my prejudices, my predispositions, my rote answers, my previous sermons' answers or topics, has allowed God to work more directly through me, whether in preparing

---

1. Susan K. Hedahl, *Proclamation and Celebration: Preaching on Christmas, Easter and Other Festivals.* (Minneapolis: Fortress Press, 2012.) 66.

and/or delivering a sermon or in listening for God's voice or listening to others' voices. God obviously "preaches" through our natural gifts, so I am not suggesting giving up those characteristics of being a great storyteller, exuding academic excellence, or charming the congregations. It is worth asking ourselves with each sermon though, "How much of this is me and how much is God?" We believe in the incarnation and the collaborative work of humanity and the divine. We just need to *remember* to seek the Divine as we present the gospel of Jesus Christ in our own words and our own lives.

Too often, in preparing a sermon, I enter into a too familiar and too often preached piece of scripture that sets off the responses to it I have given for years. It is so tempting to preach "the great wisdom" I have learned through time. I need instead, to listen for the answer to the homiletic question my preaching professor, Dr. Brosend, is always train-ing us to ask, and I am paraphrasing, "What does the Spirit want to say to the People of God today . . . right now, in this time, in this place and circumstance?" This includes not only the circumstances in the world and community within which I preach and the congregation hears, but also my own changed circumstances and different or changed listeners since the last time I preached on the particular piece of scripture. Para-phrasing beyond anything my professor meant, I may also need to ask the homiletic and personal question, "What must I let die in order for the Risen Lord to speak through me?" I find it helpful to identify, "to confess" my predispositions and previous insights, letting go of them (letting them die) and then opening myself to the Spirit asking what God wants to say.

I offer these personal examples as only one of the many things that may have to die in order for the Spirit of God to work through us. I won-der what must die in you. I can guess part of what had to die for Peter and that might lead to insight into what may have to die in us.

I believe it was his dreams for himself and his agenda for Jesus and himself that had to die.

- His agenda for Jesus being a military and political Messiah.
- His dreams of himself being a hero who would stand up for Jesus no matter what.

- His dreams of being at the right hand of Jesus as he led the forces of righteousness against the dark side of Rome.
- His putting his foot in his mouth, speaking without listening.
- His view of the kingdom of God.

His view of himself and of Jesus had to die in order to see himself as God sees him and in order to embrace and be embraced by the risen Lord. Peter had to surrender so much in order to gain victory. It was with this emptiness of all he had held dear, that he met with the others who were feeling it too.

Imagine with me the place where the apostles gathered together, maybe in the same room they shared the intimacy of the Lord's Supper and maybe even the same room where the Holy Spirit fell with transforming power upon them at Pentecost. Imagine what they were thinking and feeling. They can barely see one another through the dense fog of guilt, shame, self-recrimination, and accusation. "Where were you when they crucified our Lord?" John could have asked, "Where were you Peter when they nailed him to the cross?" The women could have asked, "Where were you Peter when they laid him in the tomb?" Peter could have responded, "At least I was there in the courtyard when they put our Lord on trial." Where were *all* of you who fled, deserting our Lord?!"

Actually, I can imagine that Peter was not far away when they crucified our Lord. After all he had the guts to follow along in the dark into the courtyard outside where the religious authorities were questioning Jesus. I can imagine him watching from a distance, maybe on an adjoining hill, listening to the cries of agony as nails are hammered and as the cross is stood up and falls into place causing even more pain to Jesus.

Maybe he was still holding on to the slim hope that Jesus would pull it out of the bag again and that Peter's agenda would win out. Maybe, he thought the same thoughts that the bystanders verbalized, "Wait, let's see if the angels come and rescue him!" These words echoed Satan's words as he tempted Jesus to jump from the temple and as he filled Peter's mouth with, "No Jesus! Quit talking about going to the cross and dying!" Did Peter remember Jesus scolding him, "Get behind me, Satan!" Once again Peter may have been listening more to the whispers of Satan than to teachings of Jesus. I can imagine Peter holding his head in his hands and saying to himself: "No! No! No! It was not supposed to go this way. This is not the way, truth or life. I was supposed to be Jesus's right-hand man and James and John would be right behind me. John would be our PR guy and James would manage our military. Judas would be secretary of treasury and Matthew would record everything that happened. Andrew would be in charge of recruitment. Thomas would publish position papers. I can see Jesus raising a sword as he cries outs we go into battle: "Come, follow me!"

Peter is awakened by another cry. As he opens his eyes he sees another sword in the distance, one stuck into the ground with a man hanging on it. He recognizes the voice of his Lord, "It is finished!"

It is finished. All they had lived for died on that cross. All they had hoped for died on that cross. All that the apostles had shared with each other on the road with Jesus died on Golgotha. In fact, all of Peter's dreams died with Jesus on the cross. Peter felt empty, lost in despair and grief, lost in nothingness. Maybe now he was ready for the Spirit of the living God to hover over his emptiness. Maybe now, with the deafening sounds of his agendas and dreams stilled, he was ready to hear and hear and understand.

Suddenly some ladies come rushing into that foggy room and breathlessly cry out, "They have taken our Lord!" Immediately Peter and John begin a sprint of a lifetime to the empty tomb. Imagine this broken empty man running to the tomb and imagine what he is thinking on the way. "Who did this? Who took the body away?" Then he slows his pace a bit and John passes him easily. "Uh oh! What if he is risen as he said he would do? What if he *did* pull it out of the bag again? What if my Lord, my deserted Lord, my denied Lord is alive?"

Peter slows to a slight jog. "Uh-oh! What am I to do? I denied him, deserted him, denied everything about who he was and what he said. I cannot face him or myself."

Pause.

Peter and John leave the empty tomb in shock and awe and wonder. Peter leaves it in fear and trembling. The apostles gather again in the upper room and Jesus appears to them. He looks into their eyes, into their hearts. "Peace I leave you." "Do not doubt but believe." "Receive the Holy Spirit."

"Who you forgive will be forgiven." "Whoever you do not forgive, will not be forgiven."

Can you imagine Peter not offering forgiveness to anyone once he experienced the forgiveness and peace of his Risen Lord . . . once his emptiness was filled by the Holy Spirit? Can you imagine Peter at every Eucharist when the words came up, "On the night in which he was Betrayed . . . Denied . . . Deserted?" Of course, Peter would offer forgiveness to all who were troubled and heavy laden and needed refreshment because he received it from our Lord. He would, of course, offer the cleansing waters of forgiveness, a new life, a rebirth into God's love and forgiveness. Should we not do the same?!

All the apostles shared this experience that bonded them for all eternity and we too are bonded with them for all eternity. Like Peter, *let us let go* of our regrets, our agendas, our hopes and fears, our hate, our need to control, our wisdom, remembering they have all been drowned in the waters of baptism. We are a new people living in a new community of faith, forgiveness and love with new hopes. Let us live lives reflecting that Truth.

Pause.

What else must die in me and you to let God's word and God's life and God's love be spoken? Must we let die the spiritual pablum and platitudes we utter; the political mottos; the excuses in our relationship; and all sorts of things. Maybe we begin by asking God that very question. "God, what must I let go, what must die in me, in order for me to truly listen to You?" This Easter morning as we listen to the rumors of a risen Lord, what must we let die in order to be reborn; what must we take on in order to experience the Risen Lord face to face and become a new creation, maybe day after day, Sunday after Sunday?

Pause.

"Alleluia. Christ is Risen!"

"Uh-oh!" We have died with Christ!

"Uh-oh!" We are a new creation!

"Uh-oh!" We are part of the church, today, yesterday, and tomorrow!

"Uh-oh!" Now we must bring all of that to the world!

"The Lord is risen indeed!"

Pentecost

Descent of the Dove, Light Bulb, and Fire!

The light bulb comes on at Pentecost. The Light of Christ is finally lit above and within the disciples of Jesus. The disciples (hopefully that includes us!) finally have something to say about Jesus that is true, and they have the courage to say it. They also are empowered by the Hoy Spirit in words and action. Maybe the world is ready to listen as well.

Easter is about the shock, awe, and wonder of experiencing the resurrection of Jesus Christ. All Saints' Day is about the resulting church for all ages and the Baptism of Our Lord is about being baptized for a purpose, believing with a purpose, and acting with a purpose for the world. Pentecost is about the light bulb of proclamation of repentance of sins and the resurrection of our Lord and Savior Jesus Christ, by word and deed in the power of the Holy Spirit.

I grew up in the Episcopal Church. I cannot remember missing a Sunday. I can remember being hauled out due to fainting. In fact, if an acolyte did not hit the floor, it was not a real worship service! I do not remember a single sermon. I was bored. I was there. I was oblivious to one and all.

The light bulb only came on when I dropped out of college and went to work in the mountains of north Georgia and met some guys who were full of Jesus. I can remember going to church with them and they had to read the prayers from the prayer book, but since I grew up in the church, attended an Episcopal boarding school, and was the son of an Episcopal priest, I knew the words by heart. However, they knew Jesus in their heart and I did not. I was so impressed with the joy and peace of these guys I was working with, that I asked them one day at work, to lay their hands on me and pray for me. Right there in the mountains they stopped work, laid their hands upon me and I prayed, "Jesus, if you are real, come into my life!" Absolutely nothing happened and absolutely everything happened! Being a good "frozen chosen" life-long Episcopalian, I felt no emotional or even intellectual response to their prayers. However, several months later, I could look back and see that I had the peace that passes understanding. I heard the words of scripture for the first time and discovered that from all those years in church of listening to scripture, I knew the stories as well as any Southern Baptist. *The light bulb came on!* The light bulb of insight came on. The light bulb of Peace came on! The light bulb of hope came on! The light bulb of Jesus Christ came on in my life and that experience has been the pilot light of my life ever since. I finally had something to share about Jesus Christ and I am sharing it today!

We say Pentecost is the birth of the church, which if true, may mean the incubation period was the three years of walking with Jesus and that the birth pangs were Holy Week.[2] My incubation time took place sitting in those pews for years, soaking in nutrients of scripture readings and Eucharist and baptism, like a seed in the soil. My Pentecost was the day the seed died and new life sprung up through the soil of the church and the red clay of north Georgia.

- Pentecost is a time for us to reflect on where the light bulbs have been or have not been lighted in our own lives and in the churches.
- Pentecost may be the time we need to pray, "Jesus, if you are real, come into my life!"
- Pentecost is a time to walk through the disinfecting waters of the baptismal pool, remembering that we have been forgiven of our sins and made one with Christ as children of God.
- Pentecost is about empowering the disciples of Jesus to boldly proclaim that the kingdom of God has arrived in the life, death, resurrection, and ascension of Jesus Christ.
- Pentecost is about attracting followers from around the world.
- Pentecost jump starts the Acts of the Apostles up through our time and beyond.
- Pentecost is about the Holy Spirit, the promised Advocate, Holy Comforter, Counselor, Teacher.
- The Holy Spirit is teaching us more and more about Jesus Christ.
- The Holy Spirit is leading us to maturity in Christ.
- Pentecost is about the Spirit of God boldly leading us where no mainline Christians have gone before … proclaiming the gospel outside

---

2. Jesus even makes this analogy of birth pangs in the sixteenth chapter, verses 21 and 22 of the Gospel of John in his farewell address.

these doors, not just by deed, which Episcopalians do well, but by word, which we are challenged to do well.

- Pentecost calls us to do more than wait and dine in an upper room or a beautiful sanctuary and parish hall. We are baptized by water and the Spirit and fire for a reason and a purpose . . . a mission.

- Pentecost calls us to do more than talk about and remember Jesus, but to take up our cross, our calendar, our checkbook, our smartphones, and follow him.

- Pentecost calls us to step out of our comfort zone and our desire to be comfortable and risk growing spiritually as individuals and as a church and like Stephen, risk being stoned for it.

We have gained much and done much through the generations but there is much more to learn and to do from generation to generation. We need to be open to the insights and revelations of the Holy Spirit. "Creation continues," as the title to Fritz Kunkel's book implies. Our understanding of God's love and of Holy Scripture and its implications in our lives and in our world, is ever expanding, much like the ever-expanding universe, and we have the opportunity through praying, listening, and studying, individually and corporately, to be empowered and led by the Holy Spirit no less than the apostles were empowered and led by the Holy Spirit on that first day of Pentecost.

We preachers rely upon the Holy Spirit every week as we (or at least I) urgently and sometimes desperately ask the Spirit to lead us and inspire us as we prepare a sermon. Understanding that we have received the Spirit at our baptism, at our confirmation, at our ordination, at our moments of inspiration, at prayers in the mountains of north Georgia or in a house or sanctuary, and at moments of being baptized into the "lights coming on," helps us live out our baptismal vows to worship God, to serve God, to repent of our sins, and to go out to seek and serve Christ in others.

We preachers may need to pray for the Holy Spirit to descend upon us, to transform us, to set us on fire. Maybe we even have to pray, "Jesus, if you are real, come into my life!" A friend of mine who is now a member of The Episcopal Church, yet previously a Southern Baptist, asked me why we do not offer an invitation to come down and publicly accept Jesus. I started to say that it is offered with every invitation to the Lord's Table, but instead,

I said, "Maybe we ought to." I'm still too frozen a chosen person to risk that in an Episcopal church, but inviting people to kneel in prayer after a sermon and offer whatever prayer to Jesus and the Holy Spirit they want, can be done even by a lifelong Episcopalian and priest.

The Holy Spirit of wisdom, of insight, of light, of power, of gentleness, or intensity, of humor, of music, of contemplation, and of action is here and now.

- Come Holy Spirit and stir us up and make us your Church.
- Come Holy Spirit and comfort those who mourn, give rest to the weary, bless the dying, soothe the suffering, pity the afflicted, shield the joyous; and all for your love's sake.[3]
- Come Holy Spirit and gives us the words that can transform the world.

Let us pray: O God of unchangeable power and eternal light: Look favorably on your whole Church, that wonderful and sacred mystery; by the effectual working of your providence, carry out in tranquility the plan of salvation; let the whole world see and know that things which were cast down are being raised up, and things which had grown old are being made new, and that all things are being brought to their perfection by him through whom all things were made, your Son Jesus Christ our Lord; who lives and reigns with you, in the unity of the Holy Spirit, one God, forever and ever. **Amen!**[4]

All Saints' Day

Christians, yesterday and today, and most likely tomorrow, have never and will never agree upon what happens in baptism. Is original sin wiped away? Are we saved? Are we simply named or christened? Should there be infant baptism or is it reserved for only adult professions of faith?

What all Christians have agreed upon is that baptism is incorporation into the church, whether it be the local one or the Church Militant.

We receive you into the household of God. We, in baptism, are not only incorporated into the church, but are made Children of God, legal heirs,

---

3. I borrowed some words from Compline, *BCP*, 134.
4. The Ordination of a Priest, *BCP*, 528.

as Paul says, with the full rights, privileges, and duties of a member of the Body of Christ. Baptism is not only an entry to Holy Communion, but full initiation by water and Spirit into Christ's Body, the church. This is a day to remember those who have gone before through the waters of baptism; the rivers of blood of martyrs; all who have been immersed, dipped, sprinkled, and even anointed in prenatal units; and those who have helped make us who we are and who we will make who they are, from generation to generation.

The bond that God established in baptism is indissoluble, like a family. Water is thicker than blood! All Saints' Day can be a reminder that we are the saints who will inspire other saints.

We receive you into the household of God. Who is the *we*? Who is the *you*?

- *We* are all those who came before, all those in the world today and all those to come.
- *We* speak for the Church Militant (current), and triumphant, for all the children of God.
- *We* are the priesthood of all believers who welcome the newly baptized.
- *We* ordained ministers, *we* priests, *we* pastors, sprinkle, dip, immerse, submerge the children of humanity and stand with John the Baptist and Jesus in the waters of the Jordan, as they pass through the waters becoming children of God.

We receive* you *into the household of God. Who is the *you*?

- We receive *you* along with the good, the bad, the ugly, and all who have gone before and who will come after you.
- We receive *you* who know what you are doing and *you* who don't have a clue.
- We receive *you* who are just going through the motions and *you* who see this as part of your devotions.
- We receive *you* who know God, who do not know God, recognizing that all are known by God.

- We receive *you* in your sin, your questions, your imaginations, your hopes, and your fears.

Having grown up as an army brat always moving around the country, I never felt I had a hometown. I never felt I belonged in any town I lived in. I was always the new kid in town and in school because we always moved during the summers. I find myself jealous of those who know where they grew up and where they came from and I still am tempted to feel like an outsider. They are the ones who can talk about the old federal building before it was an old Sears store and before it was something else.

The one constant in my life, though, besides my family, was The Episcopal Church. Wherever we traveled and moved, we always attended The Episcopal Church. I call it my hometown. I can talk about the 1928 prayer book and the good old days when acolytes fainted at every service. I can talk about how great the Rejoice Mass was and I can sing it for you if you like. No? Well, I can also talk about how much I like the "new" BCP.

The Episcopal Church has received me wherever I lived, whenever I attended, and whatever I did. There were times I was going through the motions of devotion; times when I was seeking true devotion; times when I was devoted; and times when as a teenager who attended a boys' boarding school, looked forward to church because I would see girls; and times when I was in despair, in joy, or in wonder.

Last year, I hung up the phone (that is an ancient expression) with a saint who had a major part to play in my embracing the faith, who had the peace and joy that passes understanding.

I am who I am today because of those saints.

Who are you today because of what saints?

Who will be who they become because you are a saint?

Who will be received into the household of faith because of how you live?

What a wonderful calling for our church, which is known for being an inclusive one. We accept you regardless of your beliefs, lifestyles, politics, education, social standing, abilities, what you have done and what you will do, and you name it! *That is one of the cool things about baptizing infants. We call them blessed, good and cleansed, our brother and sister, long before we know how they will "turn out."*

I have the experience at many baptisms where time merges with time and we stand within eternity as we baptize God's heirs into the one holy catholic and apostolic church. *The font and the table are where we meet eternity.*

Sometimes I experience baptisms and Eucharist as doorways, or in modern terms and for the younger generation, portals, wormholes, wardrobes of Narnia,[5] into all times and places, into eternity.

I am not alone in this perception or experience. Listen to this comment from a commentator on the first letter of John:

> According to 1 John, the Church lives in eschatological time—
> a fluid chronology, calibrated by God,
> that embraces all that has been and will be.
> Time present and time past,
> Are both perhaps present in our future
> And time future contained in time past.[6]

It sounds like a line out of Star Trek. Not only has God knit together this group of the elect, but God has knit together his "semi-complete" Body, for God needs, wants, calls, pursues all people and all creation to his side and there is yet time and room for more.

The same water we will baptize with (we brought back water from the Jordan River) is the same water with which John baptized Jesus and yet the same water with which Ananias baptized Paul; the same water where Philip baptized the Ethiopian; the same water where three thousand were baptized on Pentecost; the same water Peter used to baptize Cornelius and his entire household; the same water that was the blood of the martyrs that washed their robes white as a baptismal gown; and the waters that cleanse you, drown you, renew you, and birth you.

We receive in you into the household of faith!

- We stand with saints, martyrs, thieves, prostitutes, kings and queens, prisoners, prophets, priests, bookkeepers, doctors, lawyers, mine workers, oil riggers, chief executive officers, and police officers.

---

5. From C. S. Lewis's *The Lion, the Witch and the Wardrobe* in the Narnia series.
6. Interpreter's Bible, 12:410.

- We stand with single parents, divorced and married, gay and straight, all genders, politicians and citizens, those at tea or at coffeeshops.
- We stand with those who inspire us to love God more, whether because they did or they did not.
- We stand with those pure of heart, the meek, the merciful, the peace-makers, the persecuted, those who grieve, those in prison, those who are simply poor or poor of spirit and those who simply thirsty or thirst after righteousness.
- We stand with the hungry, the homeless, those without healthcare, and those struggling to make ends meet.
- We stand with those who struggle to love in the midst of violence; those who struggle to forgive in the midst of great pain; and with those who struggle to have hope when they live in despair.
- We stand with those who lived lives of cowardice, anxiety, stress, ambivalent faith, as churchgoers and those who leave church, as criminals, as community organizers, as protestors, as bullies and bullied, as Republicans, as Democrats, as Liberals, as conservatives, as independents, and with those who struggled and struggle with the dark night of the soul and celebrate the beauty of holiness.
- We stand with the riotous, the righteous, the unrighteous, those who hate, those who love, those who hurt and those who are hurt . . . with all God's children.

We receive you into the household of faith. We welcome the baptized into this mess and blessedness.

- Jump in! The waters will kill you and save you.
- Jump in! The waters will burn like fire as you are cleansed from sin.
- Jump in! The waters will set you on fire for God as you are anointed with the Holy Spirit.
- We receive you into the many mansions Jesus has prepared for you.
- We receive you into the blood of martyrs and the clothing of saints.
- *We* here and now, along with all the saints of God, we who have been and we who will be, in baptism, receive you into the household of faith.

Baptism of Our Lord

"Everyone has got to serve somebody!"

Who then shall we serve? How then shall we serve?

Bob Dylan's classic lyrics, written after he became a Christian, echo throughout the story of Jesus's baptism and temptations and within our own lives: "You've got to serve somebody!" "Who or what then shall we serve and how?" We can serve God or the devil, ourselves, our families, our businesses, evil, good, our own desires, God's own desires, others' desires, and so on.

Jesus struggled with these choices immediately after his baptism, at least as reported in the synoptic Gospels. Matthew and Luke spell out some of the temptations that Jesus struggled with in a dialogue with Satan. Jesus was reinforcing a decision to answer God's call on his life.

- Jesus is tempted to serve as a bread giver, not as the Bread of Life.
- Jesus is tempted to serve as a magician, not as a physician.
- Jesus is tempted to exert power by serving himself and Satan rather than offering his life for the world to serve all humanity and God.
- Jesus is tempted to serve as a son of the devil rather than as the Son of God.

"If you are the son of God, then ..." echoes the voice of the serpent in the Garden of Eden in terms of the attempt to put doubt in the mind of Eve. Jesus faced these doubts and temptations over and over again throughout his ministry, for scripture records the following:

- Even at the cross, where he could hear the echo of Satan's voice in the voices of the bystanders, "*If* you are the son of God, call upon the angels and have them bring you down from the cross!"
- Even in the voice of one of the prisoners on the cross, "*If* you are the son of God, free yourself and us."
- Even in the voices of the religious authorities, "Show us a sign."
- Even in the voice of the Samaritan woman, "Give us this water!"
- Even in the voice of those asking, "Give us that bread."

- Even in the voice of Peter, "Quit talking about going to the cross, Jesus!" (Jesus actually responds, "Get behind me, Satan!")

I can remember a particular time in my life when I was struggling with what God wanted me to do. I actually moved into a tent with my dogs for an entire summer in the mountains of north Georgia. (I would like to say I lived a spartan life, but my best buddy, Sam Buice, who lived in a house about a half mile away, is always reminding me that not only did I have my brass bed and dresser in the large VW camper tent, but that I came up to their house for coffee almost every morning.) I would meditate in the woods and ask God, "What do you want me to do?" I heard no answer for almost the entire summer.

Now I must confess that despite my asking God what God wanted me to do, I was not thinking on how to serve God, but how whatever God chose for me would give me the most fulfillment. I imagine the disciples of Jesus may have had the same self-centered reasons for leaving their nets and families in order to answer Jesus's call to follow him.

I have clearly heard the voice of God within my heart, mind, and soul only a few times in my life, and I did hear God's voice near the end of that summer. I heard God say to me, "Jim, I don't care what you do! You decide what *you* want to do and I will be with you always!" I decided I wanted to be a priest.

You will notice that God did not tell Jesus what to do at his baptism or in the wilderness, yet Jesus offered his life to the Father for the world every moment, even as he faced temptations all the way there.

So much of what happened with Jesus in baptism, happens with us in baptism.

- The Holy Spirit alighted upon Jesus in the form of a dove. We, the baptized, have been sealed by the Holy Spirit in baptism and marked as Christ's own forever. God will be with us always.
- Jesus is tempted by Satan to serve him rather than God. Temptation is intimately connected to baptism.
  - We the baptized, deal with temptations to serve ourselves rather than God.

- We the baptized, are tempted to settle for ordinary life rather than an extraordinary and sacrificial life.
- We the baptized, are tempted to be baptized and check it off our bucket list rather than fill the buckets of others.

- Jesus begins his ministry immediately after his baptism. Ministry in the kingdom of God is intimately connected to baptism. The five baptismal vows, recited throughout our lives, call the baptized to ministry.
- Jesus is declared the Son of God at his baptism. Being made a child of God, an heir to the kingdom of God, is intimately connected to our baptism.

Our connection to Jesus's own baptism reminds us that we are children of God, heirs to the kingdom of God, with all rights, privileges, and duties that come with that responsibility. The rights and privileges include reception of the Holy Spirit, being redeemed, and being empowered for ministry. We in fact will find ourselves, our fulfillment, our very lives in offering ourselves in service to God, in whose service is perfect freedom! We spell out that service in the duties of the baptismal vows. Our duties include:

- Continuing in the apostles' teaching and fellowship, the breaking of the bread, and the prayers . . . showing up at church with open minds and hearts, being open to formation and transformation.
- Resisting evil and repenting when we fall into temptation.
  - Regular confession, examining ourselves, and changing our ways as needed.
  - Not only resisting temptation but confessing when we fall into sin.
  - Confessing how often we choose to serve and build our own kingdoms rather than serve and build God's kingdom. Jesus calls us to the path less traveled, the way of the cross, and some of us may take the path of least resistance, the way of success, power, addiction, consumption, judgement, self-centeredness, and denial.
- Proclaiming by word and example the Good News of God in Christ. We proclaim that news by living lives of praise and thanksgiving and sacrifice everywhere we live and move and have our being. We proclaim

by both what we do and do not do, and what we say and do not say, including on social media and to our friends and family.

- Seeking and serving Christ in all persons, loving our neighbors as ourselves. These are active verbs and are about actively seeking Christ and seeking to serve all people.
- Striving for justice and peace among all people and respecting the dignity of every human being. That means having civil discourse around politics and other hot topics. It means addressing injustice wherever we encounter it, whether on the job, in school, in church, on social networks, in politics, and especially within ourselves.

The baptism of Jesus calls us as children of God to take up our cross and follow God. We as heirs to the kingdom and to the cross, are called to seek God's kingdom first in our lives. Striving to fulfill the baptismal vows will help keep our eyes and hearts seeking the kingdom. Remembering or simply understanding ourselves as a child of God may help us to make great efforts in living in the kingdom of God and in the world.

Reality is that most of us, including myself, are wrapped up more in our own personal kingdoms, whether they be family, work, school, or something else. We "professional ministers" can get so wrapped up in "church work" that we may forget to be about God's work. We priests have ordination vows in addition to our baptismal vows. Are we keeping them?

God sometimes gets our leftovers at best . . . leftovers of time, money, energy, vision, and passion. The vows said when we renew our vows, are not necessarily a road map for ministry but more a thermometer to help us get a sense of our baptismal spiritual health.

Baptisms or renewing our vows on the feast of the Baptism of Our Lord reminds those of us who were baptized as infants or before the "age of reason" to remember that baptism is not simply a membership ritual, but a launching pad for ministry in and through the church. Like Jesus who had not yet begun his ministry or "proven" himself, we declare infants at baptism as beloved children of God. Not only do we vow to support them in their life in Christ, but we reaffirm in the baptismal vows, the calling within baptism to ministry in the world. Jesus during his baptism received the Holy Spirit, not to simply sit in the waters and bask in his Father's approval, but to be driven by that same Holy Spirit into the wilderness and back into the "world" where he continued to wrestle with how he would serve and how he would minister, how he would live and how he would die.

Every baptism and/or renewal of our vows in this church can remind us to serve the world. How then shall you and I serve? Is there a ministry within this church you want to join? Is there a ministry within your heart that we can support? Is there a ministry in the world that is calling you? Baptisms are opportunities for you and me to ask the Holy Spirit to lead us not into temptation but into ministry.

Come on and jump in with both feet, with all your heart, mind, soul, might, and body. Get not only your feet wet, but yourselves, your souls and bodies. Ask God for guidance on doing God's work and we will transform the world!

Amen!

Bibliography

Adolph, Adam. *The Liturgical Year: Its History and Meaning after the Reform of the Liturgy.* New York: Pueblo, 1981.

Alexander, J. Neil, ed. *With Ever Joyful Hearts: Essays on Liturgy and Music Honoring Marion C. Hatchett.* New York: Church Publishing, Inc., 1999.

Alexander, J. Neil. *Celebrating Liturgical Time.* New York: Church Publishing, Inc., 2014.

Allen, O. Wesley Jr. *Preaching and Reading the Lectionary: A Three Dimensional Approach to the Liturgical Year.* Danvers, MA: Chalice Press, 2007.

Anderson, James D., and Ezra Earl Jones. *Ministry of the Laity.* San Francisco: Harper & Row, 1983.

Associated Parishes. *Holy Baptism: A Liturgical and Pastoral Commentary.* Alexandria, VA: 1991.

———. *Burial of the Dead: A Commentary.* Alexandria, VA, 1991.

———. *The Catechumenate: Formation for Church Membership.* Alexandria, VA, 1991.

———. *Holy Orders: The Ordination of Bishops, Priests and Deacons.* Alexandria, VA, 1991.

———. *Liturgy and Mission.* 1997 revision, printed from online. Alexandria, VA, 1997.

Authorized Services, 1973. New York: Church Hymnal Corporation, 1973.

Barth, Karl. *The Teaching of the Church regarding Baptism.* London: SCM Press, 1956.

Baptism, Eucharist and Ministry, 25th Anniversary Printing, Faith and Order Paper No. 111. Geneva: World Council of Churches, 2007.

Beeley, Christopher A., and Joseph H. Britton, eds. "Introduction: Toward a Theology of Leadership." *The Anglican Theological Review.* Winter, 2009, Vol. 91, Number 1. Evanston, Illinois: The Anglican Theological Review, Inc., (2009): 3–10.

The Book of Common Prayer and Administration of the Sacrament and Other Rites and Ceremonies of the Church. New York: The Church Pension Fund, 1945.

The Book of Common Prayer and Administration of the Sacrament and Other Rites and Ceremonies of the Church. New York: The Seabury Press, 1979.

The Book of Common Prayer, Church of Ireland. Dublin: The Columbia Press, 2004.

The Book of Common Worship. Louisville, KY: Westminster John Knox Press, 2018.

The Book of Occasional Services. New York: The Church Hymnal Corporation, 1979.

Bradshaw, Paul. *Companion to Common Worship, Vol. 1.* London: SPCK, 2001.

Bray, Gerald, ed. *Ancient Christian Commentary on Scripture. New Testament, Vol. VII, 1–2 Corinthians.* Downers Grove, IL: InterVarsity Press, 1999.

———. *Ancient Christian Commentary on Scripture, New Testament, Vol. VI, Romans.* Downers Grove, IL: InterVarsity Press, 1998.

———. *Ancient Christian Commentary on Scripture. New Testament, Vol. VIII, Galatians, Ephesians, Philippians.* Downers Grove, IL: InterVarsity Press, 1999.

Brockopp, Daniel C., Brian L. Heige, and David G. Truemper, eds. *Institute of Liturgical Studies Occasional Papers.* Valparaiso, IN: Institute of Liturgical Studies, 1981.

Brosend, William. *The Preaching of Jesus: Gospel Proclamation, Now and Then.* Louisville, KY: Westminster: John Knox Press, 2010.

Brownson, James V. *The Promise of Baptism: An Introduction to Baptism in Scripture and the Reformed Tradition.* Grand Rapids, MI: William E. Eerdmans, 2007.

Buttrick, David. *Homiletic, Moves and Structures.* Philadelphia: Fortress Press, 1987.

Campbell, Dennis G. *Congregations as Learning Communities.* Herndon, VA: The Alban Institute, 2000.

Chapman, Donald. "The Eight Faces of Baptism." Doctor of Ministry Thesis, Divinity School of Vanderbilt University and the School of Theology of the University of the South, 1984.

Childers, Jana. *Performing the Word, Preaching as Theatre.* Nashville: Abingdon Press, 1998.

"Common Declaration by Pope Francis and Archbishop of Canterbury Justin Welby," Episcopal News Service, *episcopaldigitalnetwork.com*, October 5, 2016, accessed October 5, 2016.

Common Worship, Services and Prayers for the Church of England. London: Church House Publishing, 2000.

Craddock, Fred B. *As One Without Authority.* St. Louis, MO: Chalice Press. 2001.

———. *Overhearing the Gospel.* St. Louis, MO: Chalice Press, 2002.

———. *Preaching.* Nashville: Abington Press, 1985.

Cross, F. L., ed. *Oxford Dictionary of the Christian Church.* Oxford: Oxford University Press, 1997.

DeSilva, David A. *Sacramental Life: Spiritual Formation Through the Book of Common Prayer.* Downers Grove, IL: InterVarsity Press, 2008.

Dix, Dom Gregory. *The Shape of The Liturgy.* Glasgow: University Press, 1954.

Douglas, Ian. "Baptized Into Mission: Ministry and Holy Orders Reconsidered." *Sewanee Theological Review.* Vol. 40, Number 4 (1997): 431–443.

Dozier, Verna J. *The Dream of God, A Call to Return.* Cambridge: Cowley Publications, 1991.

The Draft Proposed Book of Common Prayer and Other Rites and Ceremonies. New York: The Church Hymnal Corporation, 1976.

Eastman, Theodore. *The Baptizing Community.* New York: Morehouse Publishing, 1990.

Edwards, Dan. *Study Guide to Prayer Book Spirituality.* New York: The Church Hymnal Corporation, 1990.

Fenhagen, James C. *Mutual Ministry, New Vitality for the Local Church.* San Francisco: Harper & Row, 1977.

Fowler, James W. *Becoming Adult, Becoming Christian: Adult Development and Christian Faith.* San Francisco: Harper, 1984.

———. *Stages of Faith: The Psychology of Human Development and the Quest for Meaning.* San Francisco: Harper and Row, 1981.

Friedman, Edwin. *A Failure of Nerve, Leadership in the Age of the Quick Fix.* Edited by Margaret Treadwell and Edward Beal. New York: Seabury Books, 2007.

Gallagher, Nora, *Practicing Resurrection, A Memoir of Work, Doubt, Discernment, and Moments of Grace.* New York: Vintage Books, 2004.

Galley, Howard E. *The Ceremonies of the Eucharist, A Guide to Celebration.* Cambridge: Cowley Publications, 1989.

Gilbert, Charles Mortimer. *Services For Trial Use.* New York: The Church Hymnal Corporation, 1971.

Giles, Richard. *Creating Uncommon Worship: Transforming the Liturgy of the Eucharist.* Norfolk: Canterbury Press, 2004

———. *Re-pitching the Tent, the Definitive Guide to Re-Ordering Church Buildings for Worship.* Collegeville, MN: The Liturgical Press, 1999.

———. *Times and Seasons, Creating Transforming Worship Throughout the Year.* New York: Church Publishing, 2008.

———. *We Do Not Presume, A Beginner's Guide to Anglican Life and Thought.* Norwich: Canterbury Press, 1998.

Graves, Mike. *The Sermon as Symphony: Preaching the Literary Forms of the New Testament.* Valley Forge: Judson Press, 1997.

Hatchett, Marion J. *Commentary on the American Prayer Book.* San Francisco: Harper Collins, 1980.

———. Commentary on the American Prayer Book. San Francisco: Harper Collins, 1980.

———. "The Rite of 'Confirmation' in The Book of Common Prayer and in Authorized Services 1973," Anglican Theological Review, Vol. LVI, Number 3 (July 1974): 292–310.

Heath, Gordon L. and James Dvorak, eds. *Baptism: Historical, Theological and Pastoral Perspectives.* Eugene, OR: Pickwick Publications, 2009.

Hedahl, Susan K. *Proclamation and Celebration: Preaching on Christmas, Easter and Other Festivals.* Minneapolis: Fortress Press, 2012.

Hilkert, Mary Catherine. *Naming Grace: Preaching and the Sacramental Imagination*. New York: The Continuum Publishing Company, 1997.

Haskel, Marilynn L., and Clayton L. Morris, eds. *As We Gather To Pray: An Episcopal Guide To Worship*. New York, Church Hymnal Corporation, 1996

Hauerwas, Stanley, and William H. Willimon. *Resident Aliens: A Provocative Christian Assessment of Culture and Ministry for People Who Know that Something Is Wrong*. Nashville: Abington Press, 1989.

Holland, Thomas P., and William L. Sachs. *The Zacchaeus Project: Discerning Episcopal Identity at the Dawn of the New Millennium*. New York: The Episcopal Church Foundation, 1999.

Irvine, Christopher, ed. *They Shaped Our Worship*. London: Society for Promoting Christian Knowledge, 1998.

———. *The Use of Symbols in Worship: Alcuin Liturgy Guides*. London: SPCK, 2007.

Johnson, Maxwell E. *The Rites of Christian Initiation*. Collegeville, MN: The Liturgical Press, 1999.

———. *Sacraments and Worship, the Sources of Christian Theology*, Louisville, KY: Westminster John Knox Press, 2012.

Johnson, Maxwell E., and Aidan Kavanagh, eds. *Living Water, Sealing Spirit*. Pueblo: Pueblo Books, 1995.

Johnson, Trygve David. *The Preacher as Liturgical Artist: Metaphor, Identity and the Vicarious Humanity of Christ*. Eugene, OR: Cascade Books, 2014.

———_. *The Shape of Baptism, The Rite of Initiation*. Collegeville, MN: Liturgical Press, 1978.

Long, Thomas G. *Preaching from Memory to Hope*. Louisville, KY: Westminster John Knox Press, 2009.

Kavanagh, Aidan. *Elements of Rite: A Handbook of Liturgical Style*. New York: Pueblo, 1982.

Kegan, Robert, and Lisa Laskow Lahey. *How the Way We Talk Can Change the Way We Work*. San Francisco: Jossey-Bass, 2001.

Kung, Hans. *Why Priests?* New York: Doubleday, 1972.

Larive, Armand. *After Sunday, A Theology of Work*. New York: Continuum International Publishing Groups Inc., 2004.

Lee, Jeffrey. *The New Church's Teaching Series*. Vol. 7: *Opening the Prayer Book*. Cambridge: Cowley Publications, 1999.

Marshall, John S. *Hooker's Polity in Modern English*. Sewanee: The University Press at the University of the South, 1950.

Meeks, Blair Gilmer. *Seasons of Ash and Fire: Prayers and Liturgies for Lent and Easter*. Nashville: Abingdon Press, 2003.

Meyers, Gilly. *Using Common Worship: Initiation: A Practical Guide to the New Services*. London: Church House Publishing, 2000.

Meyers, Ruth, and Leonel Mitchell. *Praying Shapes Believing: A Theological Commentary on the Book of Common Prayer.* New York: Seabury Press, 2016.

Meyers, Ruth, ed. *Baptism and Ministry.* New York: The Church Hymnal Company, 1994.

Meyers, Ruth. *Continuing the Reformation, Revisioning Baptism in the Episcopal Church.* New York: Church Publishing, 1990.

Meyers, Ruth, ed. *Baptism and Ministry.* New York: The Church Hymnal Company, 1994.

Michno, Dennis C. A Priest's Handbook: The Ceremonies of the Church. Harrisburg: Morehouse Publishing, 1983.

Mitchell, Leonel. *Lent, Holy Week, Easter and the Great Fifty Days: A Ceremonial Guide.* Cambridge: Cowley Publications, 1996.

———. *Liturgical Change: How Much Do We Need?: With a Guide for Group Discussion.* New York: Seabury Press, Inc., 1975.

———. *Planning the Church Year.* Harrisburg: Morehouse Publishing, 1991.

———. *Praying Shapes Believing: A Theological Commentary on the Book of Common Prayer.* Chicago: Winston Press, 1985.

Morris, Clayton L. *Holy Hospitality, Worship and the Baptismal Covenant.* New York: Church Publishing, 2005.

Mosher, Lucinda. *Belonging, Faith in the Neighborhood, Understanding America's Religious Diversity.* New York: Church Publishing Inc., 2005.

Moule, C.F.D. *Worship in the New Testament.* Richmond, VA: John Knox Press, 1961.

The New Oxford Annotated Bible with Apocrypha, Revised Standard Version. New York: Oxford University Press, 1977.

The New Interpreter's Bible, Volume X. Nashville: Abingdon Press, 2002.

The New Interpreter's Bible, Volume XI. Nashville: Abingdon Press, 2000.

The New Interpreter's Bible, Volume XII. Nashville: Abingdon Press, 1998.

The New Interpreter's Bible, Volume X. Nashville: Abingdon Press, 2002.

A New Zealand Prayer Book. Auckland: Collins, 1989.

Nichols, Bridgett. *Liturgical Hermeneutics: Interpreting Liturgical Rites in Performance.* Frankfurt am Main: Peter Lang, 1996.

———. *Liturgical Hermeneutics: Interpreting Liturgical Rites in Performance.* Frankfurt am Main: Peter Lang, 1996.

Nouwen, Henri J. M. *Creative Ministry.* New York: Image Books, 1971.

O'Conner, Elizabeth. *Call to Commitment.* San Francisco: Harper & Row, 1963.

Quivik, Melinda. *Preaching Baptism through Lent.* Workingpreacher.org: February 6, 2012.

Rahner, Karl. *Meditations on the Sacraments.* New York, Seabury Press, 1977.

The Revised Common Lectionary, Episcopal Edition, New Revised Standard, 3 Year Cycle. Wichita: St. Mark's Press, 1992.

Russell, Joseph P. *Sharing Our Biblical Story: A Guide to Using Liturgical Readings as the Core of the Church and Family Education*. Wilton, CT: Morehouse-Barlow, 1979.

———, ed. *The New Prayer Book Guide to Christian Education*. Cambridge: Cowley Publications, 1996

Schneider, Johannes. *Baptism and Church in the New Testament*. London: The Carey Kingsgate Press Ltd., 1957.

Services for Trial Use: Authorized Alternatives to Prayer Book Service. New York: The Church Hymnal Corporation 1971.

Shattuck, Cynthia L., and, Fredrica Harris Thompsett, eds. *Confronted by God: The Essential Verna Dozier*. New York: Seabury Books, 2006.

Shepherd, Massey Hamilton. *The Living Liturgy*. New York: Oxford University Press, 1946.

———. *Liturgy and Education*. New York: Seabury Press, 1965.

Shumard, James Bradley. *A Baptismal Model for Ministry in the Episcopal Church: Connecting Liturgy, Baptism and Ministry Year-round in Ways which Are Congruent with the Book of Common Prayer in Order to Remind the Baptized of Their Baptismal Ministry*. Cambridge: Episcopal Divinity School, 2010.

Snow, John. *The Impossible Vocation: Ministry in the Mean Time*. Cambridge: Cowley Publications, 1988.

Southcott, E. W. *Receive This Child*. London: A. R. Mowbray & Co., 1951.

Spencer, Bonnell. *Ye Are the Body*. Lebanon, PA: Sowers Printing Co, 1950.

Spinks, Bryan. *Reformation and Modern Rituals and Theologies of Baptism: From Luther to Contemporary Practices*. New Haven, CT: Yale University, 2006.

Standing Liturgical Commission of the Episcopal Church. *Prayer Book Studies 18, "On Baptism and Confirmation."* New York: The Church Pension Fund.

Standing Liturgical Commission of the Episcopal Church. *Prayer Book Studies 17, "The Liturgy of the Lord's Supper," A Revision of Prayer Book Studies 4*. New York: The Church Pension Fund, 1966.

Stevenson, Peter K., and Stephen I. Wright. *Preaching the Atonement*. Louisville. Westminster John Knox Press, 2010.

———. *Preaching the Incarnation*. Louisville: Westminster John Knox Press, 2010.

Stevick, Daniel B. *By Water and the Word: The Scriptures of Baptism*. New York: Church Publishing, Inc., 1997.

———. *Baptismal Moment; Baptismal Meaning*. New York: The Church Hymnal Corporation, 1987.

Stookey, Laurence. *Baptism: Christ's Art in the Church*. Nashville: Abingdon Press, 1982.

Suchocki, Marjorie Hewitt. *The Whispered Word: The Theology of Preaching*. St. Louis, MO: Chalice Press, 1999.

Talley, Thomas. *The Origins of the Liturgical Year.* Collegeville, MN: Liturgical Press, 1991.

Tammany, Klara. *Living Water: Baptism as a Way of Life.* New York: Church Publishing Inc., 2002.

Taylor, Nicholas. *Paul on Baptism: The Theology, Mission and Ministry in Context.* London: SCM Press, 2016.

Tisdale, Leonora Tubbs. *Prophetic Preaching, A Pastoral Approach.* Louisville, KY: Westminster John Knox Press, 2010.

Turabian, Kate L. *A Manual for Writers of Research Papers, Theses, and Dissertation.* Chicago: The University of Chicago Press, 2003.

Turrell, James. *Celebrating the Rites of Initiation: A Practical Ceremonial Guide.* New York: Church Publishing, Inc., 2013.

Thompsett, Fredrica Harris. *We Are Theologians, Strengthening the People of God.* New York: Church Publishing, Inc., 2004.

Thurian, Max, and Geoffrey Wainwright, eds. *Baptism and Eucharist: Ecumenical Convergence in Celebration.* Geneva: WCC Publications, 1983.

Wainwright, Geoffrey, and Karen Westerfield Tucker, eds. *The Oxford Dictionary of Christian Worship.* New York: Oxford Univ. Press, 2006.

Wallace, James A. *Preaching to the Hungers of the Heart: The Homily on the Feast and Within the Rite.* Collegeville, MN: The Liturgical Press, 2002.

Watkins, Clare. *Living Baptism: Called Out of the Ordinary.* London: Dartman, Longman & Todd, 2006.

Webber, Christopher L. *The Vestry Handbook.* Harrisburg, PA: Morehouse Publishing, 1988.

Weil, Louis. *Christian Initiation: A Theological and Pastoral Commentary on the Proposed Rites.* Alexandria, VA: Associated Parishes, Inc., 1991.

———. *The New Church's Teaching Series, Theology of Worship.* Cambridge, Massachusetts: Cowley Publications, 2002.

———. "The Shape of Liturgical Formation: Vertical/Horizontal, Horizontal/Vertical." *Sewanee Theological Review Vol.* 52.1. (2008): 33–47.

Westerhoff, Caroline A. *Calling, A Song for the Baptized.* Cambridge: Cowley Publications, 1994.

Westerhoff, John H. III. *Bringing Up Children in the Christian Faith.* San Francisco: Harper & Row, 1980.

Whitaker, E. C. *Documents of the Baptismal Liturgy.* London: SPCK, 1970.

Williams, Rowan. *Being Christian, Baptism, Bible, Eucharist, Prayer.* Grand Rapids: William B. Eerdmans Publishing Company, 2014.

Willimon, William. *Interpretation Series, Acts.* Atlanta, GA: John Knox Press, 1988.

———. *Proclamation and Theology.* Nashville: Abington Press, 2005.

————. *Remember Who You Are: Baptism, a Model for Christian Life.* Nashville: The Upper Room, 1980.

Witherington, Ben III. *Troubled Waters: The Real New Testament Theology of Baptism.* Waco, TX: Baylor University Press, 2007.

Wood, Susan. *Ecumenical Dimensions of the Doctrine of Baptism.* Collegeville, MN: Liturgical Press, 2009.

World Council of Churches. *Lima Text on Baptism, Eucharist and Ministry.* 1982.

Yates, Arthur S. *Why Baptize Infants? A Study of the Biblical, Traditional and Theological Evidence.* Norwich: The Canterbury Press, 1993.

Zabriskie, Stewart C. *Total Ministry, Reclaiming the Ministry of God's People.* Bethesda, MD: The Alban Institute, 1995.

Acknowledgments

I want to thank Fredrica Thompsett not only for listening to my first doctoral thesis but also for reviewing this book.

I want to acknowledge the late liturgical scholars, Marion Hatchett and Lee Mitchell. Their personal conversations with me inspired me to continue down the path of baptismal values in the liturgy. Professor Mitchell emailed me a draft of his autobiography, which gave me great insight into the processes around the formation of the 1979 initiation rites.

I would like to thank Eve Strillacci and Ryan Masteller of Church Publishing for helping me to edit this book, zeroing in on the central ideas and reducing redundancy. I am a preacher, after all.

I want to thank Don Saliers and Martin Smith, two of my doctor of ministry professors who greatly influenced and inspired me. I am indebted to the scholarship and liturgical passion of Ruth Meyers, especially regarding the history and theology of baptism, and I am indebted to Jim Turrell for his scholarship regarding the full and practical aspects of the rite of baptism itself.

I want to thank Steve Kurtz for meeting with me over nine months to review every part of the manuscript. In fact, I made a couple of revisions based on his suggestions. I want to thank Jeanne Miller for reviewing it for grammatical improvements.

I want to thank Professor Bill Brosend from Sewanee for helping me with my second doctoral thesis on preaching baptism.

About the Author

The Rev. Dr. James Bradley Shumard is an ordained Episcopal priest who has served congregations for the last twenty-five years. He is also the son of an Episcopal priest. He has served in the Diocese of Atlanta, the Diocese of Georgia, and the Diocese of Wyoming.

Shumard has an ecumenical educational background. He graduated from St. Andrew's Episcopal High School in Sewanee, Tennessee, and received a bachelor's degree in religion from Rhodes College (Presbyterian), along with some studies at Cumberland Presbyterian seminary. He received a master of divinity from Candler School of Theology (Methodist) at Emory University. In 2010 he received a doctor of ministry in liturgy and congregational development from Episcopal Divinity School and a doctor of ministry in preaching in 2018 from Sewanee School of Theology (Episcopal).

CPSIA information can be obtained
at www.ICGtesting.com
Printed in the USA
JSHW060525150523
41517JS00001B/1